Of Finnish Ways

Of Finnish Ways

by Aini Rajanen

PERENNIAL LIBRARY

Harper & Row, Publishers
New York, Cambridge, Philadelphia, San Francisco
London, Mexico City, São Paulo, Singapore, Sydney

Photos courtesy of the Embassy of Finland; the Finland National Tourist Office; and *The Saint Paul Pioneer Press/Dispatch*.

A hardcover edition of this book is published by Dillon Press, Inc. It is here reprinted by arrangement.

First BARNES & NOBLE BOOKS edition published 1984.

Library of Congress Cataloging in Publication Data

Rajanen, Aini.
  Of Finnish ways.

  Originally published: Minneapolis, Minn. : Dillon Press, c1981.
  Bibliography: p.
  Includes index.
  1. Finland. I. Title.
DL1012.R35   1984   948.97   83-48378
ISBN 0-06-092382-2

---

93 94 95 MPC 10 9 8 7 6 5 4 3 2

CONTENTS

1. Suomi, Land of Contrasts 7

2. Of Lakes, Forests, and City Streets 13

3. First the Finns Were Swedes 23

4. Reluctant Russians 35

5. The Finns Are Finns at Last 41

6. The Framework of Freedom 51

7. Finland's National Scrapbook 61

8. The Dispossessed 75

9. The Flame of Faith 85

10. Medicine, Folk and Otherwise 95

11. Sometimes Gold Is Green 103

12. More Finnish Magic 113

13. Some Like It Hot 123

14. The Challenge Is Personal 135

15. Out of Their Minds 145

16. Folkways 155

17. Celebrations 163

18. Good Taste 173

19. An Orphan Language 197

20. They Came in Peace 207

Appendix: Finn Facts 214

Selected Bibliography 217

Index 219

Finland's lake district, where thousands of lakes and their wooded islands make a jigsaw puzzle of land and water.

Chapter 1

SUOMI, LAND OF CONTRASTS

IF YOU WERE TO ASK an average American what he or she knows about Finland, you would probably be told that it is a small country, uncomfortably near the Soviet Union, peopled by an enigmatic race with a great propensity for silence. You might be told other things also, but it is all too likely that they would be, well, half-truths.

Suppose you were to take a small test on Finland, right now. Would your response to these questions be true or false?

1. Finland is a part of Scandinavia.
2. Finland lies near the Arctic Circle and is very cold.
3. Finland fought against the United States in World War II.
4. Finns are blond, blue-eyed, stocky people.
5. Finland is a new country.

All of your answers are wrong, and yet all of them are right, too. Confusing? Not really. It can all be explained.

Surprising? To those who know Finns, it's not surprising at all. It merely points up one aspect of Finnish nature that is basic to understanding the cultural ways of the Finns: Finland is a land of paradox, where nothing may be taken for granted and the impossible happens all the time.

Even the country's name is a contradiction. Finland, we think, means land of the Finns. After all, Scotland is the land of the Scots, and Deutschland the land of the Deutsch. But it isn't Finn-land at all, but Fen-land—land of fens and marshes. Believing the Finns to be a race of bogtrotters, historians fastened the name on them as early as the first century A.D. To the Finns themselves, their country is Suomi, which, it must be confessed in all fairness, means "swampy." So the Finns are not Finns at all except when they are away from home. They call themselves Suomalainen.

Is this misty, marshy land a part of Scandinavia? Yes and no.

To begin with, the term "Scandinavia" is a misnomer. Purists insist there is no such place. It is not a land in itself, but a collection of characteristics that describes certain lands and peoples of northern Europe. "Scandinavian," yes; "Scandinavia," no. That last *n* makes all the difference.

Although the Scandinavian countries may be geographically similar, they can't be lumped together. At this time Finland is the least socialistic of all of them, and the only one that is not a monarchy. Its language, too, is strikingly different from the others. A Dane may manage to understand a Swede or Norwegian, but a Finn speaking Finnish might as well be conversing in Swahili!

Neither is Finland like the country bordering it on the east, the great sprawling land of Russia. Culturally there is a vast gulf. The Russian Cyrillic alphabet is no more clear to the Finn than the Greek from which it sprang. The state church under the czars was the Russian version of the Eastern Orthodox, from which the Roman Catholic Church broke away in 1054, and its rich panoply was opposed to the stern Lutheranism of Finland. Politics and history divide the two nations even more vigorously than their different cultural heritages. After a century of Russian domination, anticommunism is the essence of Finnish patriotism.

In climate, Finland is again a land of contradictions. Next

to Iceland, it is the northernmost country in the world.
Indeed, one-third of Finland lies above the Arctic Circle,
with its lower areas near the sixtieth parallel. This puts it in
the same general latitude as the mainland of Alaska.

Because of its location, most of Finland has snow five
months of each year and shares the winter temperatures of
Maine and Vermont. The upper reaches are no barren,
snow-covered waste, however, but a land where people live
and work. Forty percent of the world's people living above
the sixtieth parallel are in Finland. This is due to the warm
waters of the Gulf Stream that wash into the Baltic Sea,
thereby moderating the climate. Average temperatures in
Helsinki are 16 degrees F. in February and 63 degrees F. in
July. And in Lapland, the fabled northern sector, seventy-
three days of continuous sun bring hot summer weather to
the land of moss and lichens.

The Finns' role in World War II is equally contradictory.
When attacked by Russia in 1939, they had no choice but to
defend themselves. That put them on the opposite side of the
Allies, although they did not actively support Germany. At
the war's end, a condition of the peace was that Finland
must remove the Germans from its territory. The Finns did
so, in a bitter struggle that laid waste to much of their
country from Rovaniemi north. So in the long run, Finland
was on both sides during the war. An irony is that it was
treated as an enemy by all and had effective help from none.

We cannot even safely characterize the appearance of the
Finns, though we are on firmer ground here. It is true that
about 70 percent of the Finns fit the stereotype. There is
also, however, a goodly sprinkling of Swedish and Lapp
blood, along with some contributed by traders from
Germany, soldiers from Napoleon's fleeing army, invading
Russians, and others, so that Finns now come in all sizes
and colors. Yet they are alike in their insistence that they are

Finns. Tall or short, blond or dark, blue- or black-eyed—whatever the appearance—a Finn has something under the skin that unmistakably stamps him or her as a Finn. The word that best expresses the Finnish identity is *sisu*.

It is not surprising that sisu is a word that can't be translated. No other language has a word which quite conveys the meaning, possibly because no other country has ever had such a need of this quality. Sisu refers not to the courage of optimism, but to a concept of life that says, "I may not win, but I will give my life gladly for what I believe." It stands for a philosophy that what must be done will be done, and it is no use to count the cost. This feeling has sustained the Finns in fighting forty-two wars with Russia and losing every one. It's the quality that lets them laugh at themselves in the face of disaster. It's the hard-jawed integrity that makes them pay their war debts when wealthier nations repudiate their obligations. In short, it's the indomitable will that sets Finns apart and explains many of the incredible things they do. Sisu is the only word for the Finns' strongest national characteristic.

Our test has shown that there is yet another misconception about Finland: is it a new or an old country?

Certainly it is a new country. As a nation it is less than seventy-five years old, having been born in 1917. But it is new in other ways, too. Finland looks like a new country. There are cities, like Helsinki and Rovaniemi, that almost glisten in newness because they have been so recently rebuilt. In a land where the forest renews itself and the population is rather sparse, there is no urban sprawl or towns overrun with people. The national penchant for cleanliness and order may have something to do with this, and the enforced rebuilding and resettlement after World War II made it necessary. It's obvious to visitors that the Finns have a youthful outlook that expresses itself in planned cities and a desire to be modern.

At the same time, Finland is old. Its capital city of Helsinki was settled by royal command in 1550, and the city of Turku began as an outpost fort in 1220. The Finns themselves are an archaic people, already known by that name nearly two thousand years ago.

The land consists of the oldest surface rock known—a rock-ribbed granite that rose from the sea. The land that became Finland was formed eons ago, at a time when northern Europe was emerging from its shell of primeval ice. Through thousands of years of time, the land lay under a mantle of ice in a long sleep that lasted until 16,000 B.C.

Slowly, with the infinite patience of nature, the thaw began. The Continental Ice Sheet retreated northward, sometimes as much as four hundred yards a year. Six thousand years passed and, freed from its burden of ice, Finland began to emerge from the sea, its water pouring off and forming ridges called eskers. Another three thousand years, and Finland was free of its icy prison.

But the glacier had not been entirely a cruel mistress. In its retreat it left Finland dotted with the tens of thousands of lakes that make up its beautiful landscape today.

As the ice retreated, the granite base called the Fenno-Scandian Shield rose higher. To this day it continues to rise, and even now the province of Ostrobothnia rises about ten feet in a hundred years. Considering that the Fenno-Scandian Shield is the oldest exposed rock base in the world and rising still, Finland is at once the oldest and newest land in the world.

The more we study Finns and Finland, the more we learn to expect the unexpected. Where did they come from, these sturdy folk whom the Russians call "The Unusual People"? Why are they so different, so individual, so fiercely independent? The answer lies in their country and its history.

An outline map of Finland.

CHAPTER 2

OF LAKES, FORESTS, AND CITY STREETS

NATURE HAS BEEN LAVISH in its gifts to Finland. The land is sliced by rivers and spattered with lakes—at least sixty thousand of them. The rivers are not tame, calm waterways, but foaming torrents, teeming with fish in the unpolluted upper reaches, that dash madly toward the salt water. Then there are forests, vigorous and dense, that come right to the edges of the cities they surround. There are more than a thousand miles of island-girded coastline.

A glance at a map of Finland reveals a country backed up against the giant Soviet states of Russia and separated from the rest of Europe by two arms of the Baltic Sea: the Gulf of Finland and the Gulf of Bothnia. A physical features map of Finland is colored mostly green, signifying low-lying lands, except for the northern areas, which are tan to show slightly more rugged terrain.

Although the country has twelve provinces, their names are of little concern to anyone except a native Finn; they aren't even needed in addressing letters. For practical purposes Finland may be divided into four geographic regions, each distinctly different from the others but nevertheless a part of the composite picture that is Finland.

The traveler sees first the coastal lowlands of the southwest, the green plains that follow the 1462-mile coastline. Here are gentle hills and valleys, fertile soil, and the most moderate climate any Finns enjoy. It falls naturally that this area is the most cultivated. Naturally, too, its cultural history is the oldest. With their bustling, vigorous young cities, the southwestern lowlands are the fastest-growing region of Finland. Anyone looking for opportunity in Finland has only to see the glistening city of Helsinki to say, "This is the place!"

Farther east is the lake district of central Finland. The map shows a bewildering expanse that in places is as much water as land, a veritable jigsaw of lake, stream, and forest. The lakes and streams are dotted with thousands of little islands and connected by a labyrinth of canals to make a vacationer's paradise. Largest of all is Lake Saimaa, 680 square miles of glimmering water, the focus of a canal system that is 185 miles long. It is an anachronism to find here the nation's foremost industrial center, Tampere, neatly settled between two lakes.

All of Finland is not so blest. The upland region, north and east, is two-fifths of Finland's land area but ranks far below that in productivity and population density. It's a harsher, more inimical land, with soils that are poorer, a climate that is rugged, and a surface that is a mixture of upland and swamp. Yet here is much of the spirit that permeates Finland. The foaming, hard-to-tame rivers have been harnessed to provide energy, and the people exhibit a hardihood in keeping with their land.

There is still another part of Finland not included in these divisions, and that is the plethora of small islands off the coast. Although they number in the thousands, their combined area is only 572 square miles. Most are uninhabited; what people do live on them speak Swedish. The largest island, Ahvenanmaa (still known by its Swedish name of Åland) is 285 square miles of rocky outcrop. Though they may be used for fishing bases or summer homes, the coastal islands are of little economic importance.

On a visit to Finland, the first place you'd be likely to see would be Helsinki, the capital. It's also the largest industrial city and the most important cultural center. Eleven percent of Finland's people live here.

The heart of the city is clustered on a peninsula which juts out into the Gulf of Finland, a sea which freezes in winter but is kept open by icebreakers. Since it is also Finland's most important harbor, all avenues of Finnish life lead to Helsinki.

Often called "the White City of the North," Helsinki looks like a new city, with gleaming buildings that are the embodiment of modern architecture, clean lines, and wide streets with parklike vistas. It's actually an old city, but unlike others its age, it didn't "jest grow." Trust the Finns to come up with one of the earliest planned cities in the world.

The first city of Helsinki was planned way back in 1550 when Finland was under Swedish rule. In the hope that a new city would challenge the power of Tallinn in nearby Estonia, King Gustavus Vasa decreed that four towns should pick up their businesses, pack up their people, and move to a new spot on the rapids of the Vantaa River. Ninety years later the town moved again to its present location so that Helsinki might have a harbor. It flourished in the shadow of older cities until 1808 when it was all but destroyed by fire in the war that gave Finland to Russia.

The Finns have always had a passion for sweeping up the debris of the past and getting a new, clean start. They rebuilt Helsinki building by building, following a design by a German architect named Carl Ludwig Engel.

Meanwhile, the Russian czars looked askance at Finland's old capital of Turku, sitting uncomfortably close to their old enemies, the Swedes, who were firmly entrenched in the city's life. And so, in 1812, Helsinki became the center of Finland's government, which it has remained ever since.

Like Washington, D.C., and Brasilia, it has borne the marks of an administrative city almost from birth.

The most impressive part of the city is the Senate Square—no tourist should miss it. Here is the majestic cathedral, the State Council Building, and the University of Helsinki. Together they make an imposing grouping that sets the tone for Finland. From the time they were built, the hallmark of Finland has been architecture, and there's hardly a street in the whole country that doesn't reflect this in the clean, modern lines of its buildings.

It seems odd to find no ruins in this city of white roofs, but the seeker after history can lose himself in the Island Museum, Seurassani. Here are the bones of ancient Finland— wolf pit, tar pit, prison, Viking boat, and two longboats— with costumed caretakers in the proper regalia of the province. Also nearby is the hoary fortress of Suomenlinna (Castle of Finland), situated on a series of islands in the harbor.

No visitor should leave Helsinki without visiting the nearby garden city of Tapiola. This is a housing project so thoroughly planned it doesn't look planned at all. Reached by bridges from island to island, it is set like a jewel in parkland. In the beauty of pines and birches, flowers and fountains, its modern architecture is pleasing to the eye from every angle. In the heart of the city, you think you are in the country.

Turku is different. Finland's first major city and still third in size, Turku is the embodiment of the dark struggles of the nation's history. Dominating it is the huge fortress that has guarded the city since the thirteenth century, when Turku was founded as a gateway to the farming area. (The name of the city means trading post.) The grim, implacable look of Turku Castle fits its bloody history and brings to life grisly tales of imprisonment and torture. At one time the bones of

Saint Thomas were buried here, but in 1913 they were taken to Russia, leaving only the remains of Karen Monsdatter, an early queen, and Desirée, Count Bernadotte's lovely consort, in the castle.

From the same era is the ancient cathedral, which has been the headquarters of the archbishop of Finland for seven hundred years.

Not much remained of Turku after the disastrous fire of 1827. The blaze started from tallow candles in a butcher's shop. The wooden buildings were engulfed in flames, one after another, until only the stone buildings, such as the cathedral built by Saint Thomas, could withstand it.

One of the few parts of the old town that survived was a small street of shops kept by individual tradesmen. It was the natural setting for a handicraft museum, and that is what Turku has established there. The "museum" is actually a series of small shops like those that existed at the time of the fire, operated by costumed tradesmen who ply their trades and sell their wares. Several medieval stone churches, steeped in the old traditions, also remain. You can even see an old full-rigged ship.

Surrounded as it is by the spirit of ancient Finland, Turku surprises the traveler with its modern tourist facilities and its beautiful beach at Naantali. Handsome people in the latest beach attire contrast oddly with the remains of ancient settlements of the Åland Islands.

We have seen an administrative center and a historical center. Now let's look at Finland's chief industrial center, the city of Tampere, next in size to Helsinki.

Tampere had its beginnings in 1779, when George Rogers Clark and John Paul Jones were doing their thing in the Revolutionary War. Detroit was a fort then, and Chicago a mere hamlet. Once more, a Swedish king decided that river rapids would be a good place for a city. Those of the

Tammerkoski happened to be the spot from which expeditions to northern Finland and Lapland were launched. Tampere's industrial development began in the early 1800s when a Scotsman, James Finlayson, established a spinning mill there. It's now a weaving wonderland. Often called the Manchester of Finland, Tampere is a far cry from the smoky industrial city of England. Though there are more than four hundred factories in Tampere, the natural beauty of the city is unscarred.

The city is built around Pyynikki, a high ridge with a tower from which the stunning vista of the surrounding area may be seen. The Finns love the country deeply, and this stunningly modern, busy city is almost within a stone's throw of forests and calm lakes that soften the impact of the wheels-of-progress whirl and re-create a lyrical sylvan atmosphere.

Equally startling is the renowned Pyynikki Open Air Theater, in which the spectators revolve around the stage. Excitingly modern productions are given in a lovely natural setting. If you have a chance to see one, don't miss it. There's no danger of getting dizzy!

Finns are proud of the high standard of excellence of their products, and the functional factories reflect this even in the way they look. They are not at all the dingy, soulless structures that the word "factory" conjures up. It's symbolic of the Finnish way of life that these humming industrial complexes are set in parks with trees, fountains, and statues. In one Tampere park there's even a statue of a tax collector!

Let's take a look at Lahti, next. In the central part of Finland, it is the gateway to the lake district. It's a very new city, having been born in 1905. We'd expect it to be much like our own cities of this vintage, and the Finns themselves consider it to be the most "American" of their towns. Woodworking is its chief activity as far as commerce is concerned, but Lahti has another claim to fame—it is the mecca for winter sports. Every March a high glacial ridge that crosses the edge of town is the site of international contests in ski-jumping, cross-country skiing, and other popular events. Travelers in search of more peaceful pastimes love the area beyond Lahti, with its vast forests and uncounted lakes. Many of the lakes are joined by canals that form a waterway to make the wild and lonely countryside accessible by boat.

While we're in the lake district, we shouldn't bypass Kuopio, a city of fifty-three thousand people, which is tucked back in the bewildering hinterland of lakes and forest. A sister city to Minneapolis, Minnesota, Kuopio is about two hundred years older than her big sister in our "Land of Lakes." Only a few of its early wood houses may still be seen and the city has continued to grow and spread, but there is nothing haphazard about it. The buildings are architecturally satisfying, and a 250-foot tower perched on a 700-foot hill provides a revolving "space needle" with a lovely view of the city and its environs. The International Winter Sports Meeting, held every March, is well worth the trip. At warmer times of the year, a tourist may see rafts of floating logs, half a mile long, making their way down the lakes to market. Kuopio is also the home of *kalakukko*, a fish pie in a rye crust that is a famous Finnish delicacy.

In the hinterland beyond Kuopio is an unlikely place for a castle, but Savonlinna has the best preserved castle in Finland. Olavinlinna (Saint Olaf's Castle) was built in 1475 to protect the settlers of Finland during the wars that kept the land forever changing hands. Its once-proud five towers are now reduced to three, but one can still see the executioner's block and the justice room with the trap door. Olavinlinna was built to last, with walls twenty feet thick. Travelers are always intrigued with the *garde robe*, the restroom of the

times, built with an overhang that thrusts out over nothing-
ness. In the spirit of things, there is folk dancing in summer.

Oulu, at the northern end of the Gulf of Bothnia, is our
next stop. Wood products traveling down fast rivers from
the timbered interior pass under Oulu's sixty bridges on
their way to the city's port. In years gone by, Oulu was the
headquarters of the tar industry. The tarmakers made their
way on foot beside the wild and foaming rivers to their
headwaters in the huge evergreen forests. Here the men
spent the winter boiling out tar and resins, which they
packed in wooden barrels and loaded into the characteristic
narrow wooden boats they built. In these frail craft they ran
the rapids to the sea each spring.

The oldtime tarmakers were a rowdy lot. Local legend has
it that in one of their "games," they took turns stabbing one
another, each thrust going a measured amount deeper, to see
who would endure the longest. The residents of one village
claimed that no male was considered a man who did not dare
thrust his own knife through his hand. Among the *puukkojunkkarit*, as these knife-wielding Finns were called, knife
scars were as much a badge of honor as rapier scars were to
the duelists of Germany.

The industry dwindled with the coming of coal tar, but
there are still some old tar warehouses in Oulu, and you can
buy small replicas of the tar boats.

Continuing north, the city to watch for is Rovaniemi, only
five miles from the Arctic Circle. Nowhere in the country is
there a more lambent example of the Finnish "I-don't-quit"
spirit than Rovaniemi. After the city was leveled in World
War II, the Germans were hardly out of sight when the
inhabitants began to rebuild. Finnish custom is to build the
sauna first to provide for housing and cleanliness, then build
the barn for a livelihood, and last of all, "let the barn build
the house." And that is what the people did. As the economy

grew and expanded and the crops flourished, the building increased. Now Rovaniemi has more structures than before its destruction.

All roads intersect in Rovaniemi. Some lead to hamlets in Lapland, for Rovaniemi is considered the gateway to Lapland, though the nearest Lapp village is two hundred miles away. Lapp handicrafts may be found in Rovaniemi, and here are the winter fur markets.

Beyond lies Finland's wild North, the land that time forgot. Here is the unspoiled tranquility of solitude and silence, where commercialism has not yet destroyed a way of life that is rigorous yet gentle, primitive yet colorful.

Lapland has much to offer. There are winter sports under the Northern Lights from January to April. From December to March the reindeer roundup is held in such centers as Ivalo, Inari, and Enontekiö. During the time of the Midnight Sun, from mid-May to July, there are other activities to engage your interest: shooting the rapids near Rukatunturi, washing gold in the Lemminjoki River, fishing for salmon at Utsjoki, and watching loggers' competitions. Be warned, however, that the mosquitoes of Lapland are noiseless!

Traveling in spirit from one end of Finland to the other has given us a sample of this land of incredible contrasts. So, what is the essence of Finland? Is it the clean-lined modernity of Helsinki, or the bustle of factory-filled Tampere? Should we think of old, unhappy Turku, steeped in tradition, or Rovaniemi, where primitive culture exists cheek-by-jowl beside a new-built city? There's no answer. There's no one word for the charm of Finland, not even the charm of the unexpected. We must accept what we've been saying all along: Finland is a country of contrasts, where nothing is forced into a pattern, and "doing your own thing" was invented centuries ago.

Olavinlinna (Saint Olaf's Castle) in Savonlinna is a five-hundred-year-old reminder of Sweden's rule.

Chapter 3

FIRST THE FINNS WERE SWEDES

The rugged land of Finland has begotten a rugged people: tenacious, impervious to all attempts to change or assimilate them, and determined to be independent. Facing the constant threat of ravage by their neighbors and battling a stern land for existence, how else could they survive?

In spite of their stubborn determination to be Finns and nothing else, our Chosen People are a very difficult group for the historian to follow around. Part of this is due to the confusion they aroused in others who kept the records. Historians often called the Lapps Finns, which is understandable, but they also called the Finns Norwegians, Swedes, and even Russians. Occasionally they even called them Finns.

Another problem is that there is no case in which we can follow the adventures of an outstanding leader or hero, whose exploits are told in song and story. If there had been an Eric the Red or Alfred the Great around whom stories clustered, we might have dim pictures of life in those dark days before history dawned. Alas, the closest we have to this sort of hero is Väinämöinen. A rugged individualist like all Finns, he is not really documentable. (His story in the *Kalevala* will be dealt with in chapter 7.)

Then, too, the archeologists' task in Finland is very difficult since perishable wood was a common and favored prehistoric building material. The stone of Finland is gneiss,

which is difficult to work; it breaks into lumps and is hard to
fabricate into walls. Lacking limestone, the Finns of necessity
turned to wood as a building material. Thus, in Finland
there grew a democracy of dwellings: any man's home could
be as large and ornate as a chief's if he wanted to put forth
the effort. A king's hall as well as a commoner's hut would
fall into decay and disappear.

Evidential finds are rare. For a period of five centuries,
from A.D. 500 to 1000, there is nothing to prove whether
people lived in the area or not. But, of course, they did. By
about 700 B.C., Finland had people in three areas: Suomi, the
southwestern area, which expanded to become eventually
the dominant sector; Häme, the midsection; and Karelia, the
land bridge to the east.

There were also the Lapps, a mystery within a mystery.
No one can unravel the origins of these shy, smiling people
who inhabit the northern wastes of Norway, Sweden, and
Finland. It seems probable that they were in what is now
Finland when the present Finns got there. Gentle and
tractable, they allowed themselves to be pushed back to the
lands nobody else wanted. Poignantly, their own name for
themselves means "the banished."

Unfortunately, we have no written records of Finland
earlier than the twelfth century. But do not imagine for a
moment that this means Finland wasn't there. Such dis-
tinctively Finnish objects as a ski, a sledge runner, coins, and
bits of birch have been found. Most finds, however, date
from A.D. 1000 to 1200, towards the end of the Viking Age.
Although the Finns came out of the shadows with the
Vikings, it doesn't appear that they followed the example of
their avaricious neighbors, who harried the coastal tribes as
a national pastime. The Finns did move with the times,
however, and took advantage of the opportunity.

The flowers of Finnish culture at this time were itinerant

metalworkers, both of ornaments and weapons, and craftsmen in wood. The Finns turned these talents to account. Norwegian history tells of a ship being built by Lapps (Lapp and Finn being interchangeable terms), and there is a record of Finnish villages in Norway paying rent in the amount of a boat a year. There were also the "Sea Finns," highly skilled shipwrights and carpenters who spent part of their year on the Norwegian fjords, fashioning the sleek Viking ships. We may assume that the Finn fathers matter-of-factly went where the jobs were, working for the Vikings at their crafts, picking up a few foreign coins and ornaments as rewards, and perhaps gathering a few souvenirs for the girls on their way home. The prudent Vikings, no doubt, knew a good thing when they saw it, and forbore to rock the boat by ravaging their carpenters' homeland while the menfolk were away. At any rate, the coins and ornaments of the period that have come to light in Finland were not left behind by Viking raiders.

During this time, an entity that became known as Finland was being formed. It had a sturdy peasant society that in its almost classless structure felt no feudal need of a castle protecting every village. There were obvious differences in wealth as shown by the graves of the era. Some graves appear to be those of rich chieftains, while others are of menials. It would seem there must have been some differences in rank, for the words *kuningas* ("king") and *ruhtinas* ("prince") were part of the language, though they may not have meant quite the same then as now. Most of the people, however, were not serfs. The men had weapons and were presumably prepared to use them in defense of their homes and freedom.

The homes of the early Finns may seem crude, but they were not so different from those our pioneers made. Usually they were one-room log cabins built with timbers interlocked in the distinctive style that the Finns later brought to America. Roofs were made of birchbark weighted with sod to keep it from curling, thus serving the double purpose of preventing leaks and retaining heat. Birchbark was a craftsman's material, and the Finns used it for shoes, baskets, watercraft, and even clothing. Finns of today still work in birchbark with great skill.

They made their living by hunting, trapping, and herding. Life was not easy, and perhaps this is the key to the lack of feudal power in the hands of a lord. In a land where it was such a desperate struggle just to stay alive, what was there to tempt the robber barons of old? Whatever the reason, the Finns lived in their hamlets and on their farms, giving obedience to neither God nor man and accepting no authority except their common, unwritten law.

It seems, however, that the Finns who were away from home building ships did not leave well enough alone. They began to do a little raiding on their own, perhaps on their way home from Norway in beautiful longboats like those they had constructed for the doughty Vikings. Naturally, the handiest place to raid was the southern and eastern coast of Sweden, being right on their route, so to speak. It is not to be expected that the Swedes were very happy about this state of affairs, and no doubt the taxpayers complained to the government. Eventually, King Eric IX had had enough.

At this time in the Old World, it was quite fashionable to go on crusades for the purpose of demonstrating to erring people that they had jolly well better be good Christians, or they were going to get banged around a bit. King Eric was a Christian and eager to do what he could to spread the true religion about. What better field for a little missionary work than Finland, where his soldiers would have a chance to make well-behaved, tax-paying Christians out of a bunch of heathen pilferers? Eric decided it was his sacred duty to do a little conversion by brute force and sundry head-loppings.

This first crusade took place around 1150, and Eric followed it up by calling on Henry, an Englishman who was the bishop of Uppsala, to complete the task of conversion. But the Finns would have none of him. Eventually, to put an end to his exhortations about hell fire and some of his even more unpopular habits, a peasant named Lalli took an ax to him as he was crossing a frozen lake. Later, the Finns were sorry about this unkind treatment of a good man, and the luckless Henry was canonized. So he is now Saint Henry, the patron saint of Finland.

From this situation came the first genuinely Finnish historical document, a bull written by Pope Alexander II in 1172, in which he deplored the ungrateful, intractable behavior of the Finns in resisting Eric's heavy-handed Christianity and refusing to give up the faith of their fathers.

There are many war tales of these and subsequent years. In the province of Häme can be found the remains of a cathedral built seven hundred years ago of granite and brick, with the Bible story in pictures around its walls. This same church also has racks for weapons to be stored handily during worship and a stone for the ultimate sacrifice of those who wouldn't be converted that testifies mutely in its scars and stains to the blood that once flowed over it.

The struggle went on for seventy-five years. The zeal of the Christians was unabated by their reverses. Going as a missionary to Finland was as popular as calls to Africa became centuries later. It was popular in Finland, too. Missionaries made good slaves, and slaves were a portable commodity with certain economic value. The influx of the fervent continued and swelled until the market became glutted. The Finns tried to discourage the oversupply of missionaries by hanging them, but the Swedes continued to ship them in. Finally, another Englishman and bishop,

Thomas by name, stopped the slave trade in clerics. Putting Finland under the direct protection of the pope in 1229, he brought in so many priests, along with a good supply of soldiers, that the practical Finns saw the light.

Actually, the military aspect of the crusade had little to do with its outcome. The Finns gave in because they were ready to accept a working relationship with Sweden in defense against the Russians and because receiving the new religion was part of that relationship. The only political concession they made was to recognize Sweden's king as their own, and in an almost classless, nonfeudal society such as Finland's, there was little hardship in this.

It should be noted that although the governing authority of Finland was now Swedish, its influence did not extend to all of the territory. Birger Jarl, the Swedish king's brother-in-law, annexed a chunk of the lake district in 1249, and in 1293 the Swedes launched a crusade against neighboring Karelia, taking it over in 1323.

From the time of Swedish conquest, the fighting Finns furnished the backbone of Sweden's armies in their innumerable wars, mainly in conflict with Russia. They rallied to their new rulers with the same spirit in which the Saxons of England flocked to the banners of Richard Coeur de Leon. Similarly, legends grew up around their leaders, with Finnish magic invoked to explain their victories. One of their heroes, Knut Porse, sent the Russians flying by cooking up an explosive potion of frogs, chalk, and quicksilver. When the castle he was defending was surrounded by superior forces, he was undismayed; all he needed was a little sorcery. Climbing up on the battlements, he shook out a feather pillow. The feathers floated down, becoming armed men as they landed, and the Russians were quickly routed!

Apart from the military participation and the fact that the

national language was Swedish, the Swedes did little to subjugate Finland. The new duchy ranked equally with older provinces. True, the king handed out various sections to favored nobles. True, any Finn with ambition had to learn Swedish, but that wasn't very hard since it was taught in the schools. Much that was good, in both learning and industry, came to Finland from Sweden, including the university established at Turku by Count Per Brahe.

For their part, the Finns accepted Swedish domination without demur and followed the fortunes of their conquerors with wholehearted energy. Some Finns "Swedified" their names, and so it is sometimes difficult to separate these Finns-in-disguise from Finns with a genuine Swedish heritage.

This shared political past and cultural and religious unity has given Finnish history some of the flavor of the other Scandinavian nations. There was even a brief period when Norway, Sweden, Finland, and Denmark were all ruled as one. This period of the Three Crowns, as it is called, extended from 1388 to 1448, and the traveler in Finland can still find signs of it chiseled into the lintels of ancient entries.

The underlying cause of this strange contretemps was the old dictum that royalty must marry royalty, not only to keep the blood a purer blue, but also to add a little territory and a few taxpayers by the peaceful means of matrimony.

The royal acquisitions began when Haakon VI, the king of Norway, died and left the kingdom to his queen, Margaret of Denmark. When her father died, she also assumed the crown of her native land. Then Sweden, none too happy with the oppressive rule of Albert of Mecklenberg and his German sword, elected her their queen, also.

Naturally Albert didn't take kindly to this, and war ensued. He lost, but not before he had taken toll of his opposition for seven bloody years. Margaret further complicated matters by dying without an heir, and the battles started again. All the nations concerned turned to war as the logical way to settle matters, and Finland supplied one-third of Sweden's soldiers.

Things went from bad to worse. Matters culminated in what history refers to as the Stockholm Bloodbath of Christian II. In unnatural savagery that finally provoked the censure of the pope, Christian launched persecutions of wanton ferocity, using the wheel, the gallows, and horrible torture on whomever he conceived to be his opposition, not sparing his favorites, the clergy, or small children.

Never famous for being long suffering, the people simmered impotently until a leader arose. A young nobleman, whose male relatives were murdered and whose mother and sister had died in Christian's dungeons, escaped from custody disguised as a peasant, eluded capture, and rallied the oppressed.

Gustavus Vasa (1523–1560) was a hero of the same caliber as Bonnie Prince Charlie and Robin Hood. He narrowly escaped capture many times, once being lowered through a window by a woman while Christian's soldiers were hammering at the door, once hiding in a cartload of hay and evading his enemies by keeping silent even when jabbed with a fork. Insurgents of Sweden and Finland were swept into his forces, bound by his charismatic personality and remarkable acumen. Soon he had an army to challenge Christian's and was elected king, after which he prudently declared the monarchy to be hereditary henceforth and the heir to the crown to be known as the duke of Finland. More far-reaching effects came from his dissolving the relationship with the Catholic Church and establishing Lutheranism in Sweden/Finland in 1527.

When Gustavus's eldest son Eric took over, things were different. From the first Eric XIV showed an unstable, capricious nature. With him, suspicion was proof, and he developed a paranoic fear of many of his nobles. In this he was abetted by an astrologer who led him to sacrifice a loyal family, even forging evidence to do so. When the nobleman protested his innocence, presenting his dagger to his sovereign, the demented king stabbed him with it.

Not without vanity, Eric courted Elizabeth of England, Mary Queen of Scots, and a princess of Hesse. None of them accepted him. Ultimately, he married a beautiful Finnish girl, Karin Monsdatter, whom he saw standing on a Stockholm street corner. She alone of those near to him could quiet his insane rages.

Of his brother Johan, named co-heir with him by their father, he was endlessly suspicious, perhaps with some reason. At any rate he imprisoned Johan in the castle at Turku, and visited him several times with the intention of murdering him. Somehow he could never quite bring himself to do the deed, and eventually his nobles, no longer able to give their support to a mad king who ran about in the woods and howled, swapped him for Johan. Then Eric had his turn in the little dark cell in Turku castle, deserted by everyone except his lovely wife, until he was mysteriously poisoned.

Throughout this time and after, Sweden was continuously embroiled in wars. For sixty years of unremitting conflict, the armies of Russia and Sweden seesawed back and forth over Finland, which became known as "the Bloody Shield of Sweden."

The Finnish cavalry was noted for its ferocity. In the wars of Gustavus Adolphus, the Protestant Lion of the North, they were given "horrible mention": "From the horrible Finns, dear Lord, deliver us," prayed the trembling Catholic followers of the Hapsburgs.

On its eastern frontier, Finland was harassed by the Russians, whose armies struck at their powerful enemy across the buffer of Karelia. The eight-year period during which Russia occupied Finland, from 1713 to 1721, became known as the Great Wrath because of the terrible suffering the Finns endured. One-fourth of the Finnish population was destroyed, and Helsinki, Lappeenranta, Pietarsaari, and Porvoo were burned to the ground. The Small Wrath (1741–1743) followed before the Finns had time to recover from the effects of previous Russian occupation. This unremitting cruelty laid the foundation for Russia's being considered the hereditary enemy of Finland.

Eventually the Russian juggernaut overpowered the sons of the Vikings, and Finland was the price. In 1809 Sweden formally ceded Finland to the czar. It was the end of an era that had spanned almost six hundred years. The Finns were Swedes no more.

On balance, it's only fair to say that Sweden's rule over Finland was not all bad. A lot has been said, here and elsewhere, about Finland fighting Sweden's wars, but this was only to be expected. The king was the unquestioned leader in time of war, and all citizens had the obligation to bear arms in his defense (or offense). On a more positive note, Sweden helped Finland to develop from a primitive society into a Western European nation. It expanded the Finnish economy and stimulated foreign trade. Roads and castles were built, and Finland was supplied with a cathedral and a university as fine as Sweden's own.

Cultural development in the Scandinavian countries lagged behind the advances of the south by as much as five hundred years, according to some estimates. Though Gustavus Vasa loved and protected learning, many of his highest knights and officers were unable to read or write. In spite of a nominal Lutheranism, many old superstitions inherited from pagan times and never abolished under Catholicism remained. Nobles as well as peasants believed in witchcraft, and medicine was chiefly a matter of prayers and exorcism.

Gradually, as the Age of Enlightenment spread northward, old ways disappeared, and the gap between the Scandinavians and the Western European peoples closed. New learning and skills reached Finland through Sweden and found the people ready. Administrators who were wise rather than oppressive kept the duchy in a position befitting its rank as the one which gave titular name to the crown prince.

Neither was the yoke a galling one politically. Sweden could not legally change any Finnish law, nor enact any new tax without Finland's consent through its representatives. The property rights of the Finns and their individual freedom were respected. The only worm in the apple was that the Swedes weren't Finns.

The aristocratic ruling class was, of course, drawn from the Swedes, which meant that socially a Finn was likely to be second class. But the long period of fraternization led to a new kind of Finn, the Swede-Finn, who was Swedish in part by inheritance and yet because of his residence among Finns, wholly Finnish in patriotism. Many of Finland's greatest people, even leaders in the movement for autonomy, have been drawn from this mixture. Perhaps it was the force of the wild free land or the untamed mettle of their neighbors, but something inspired these people with the sisu of the Finn-Finns, so that they became second to none in their love of country.

Swedish was their history, Russian their new designation, but whatever their heritage, they never stopped being Finns.

National flags emblazoned with the Finnish coat of arms fly behind an equestrian statue of Carl Gustav Mannerheim.

CHAPTER 4

RELUCTANT RUSSIANS

POLITICIANS, IT SEEMS, never learn to let well enough alone in pushing around the long-suffering taxpayers.

The Finns had been Swedes for almost six centuries. They were used to the manners and customs of Swedish rule and felt that their homeland was a part of the Swedish kingdom. Resentful as they had sometimes been at being used by the kings of Sweden as a buffer, they were proud of their contribution to Sweden's military strength. They had also enjoyed political autonomy, and their rights had been respected.

Then Russia overran Finland in 1808 under a flag of truce. The Swedes were busy elsewhere and could give no help. Knowing they would lose but refusing to surrender, twelve thousand Finns fought and held an army of eighty-five thousand Russians for a year and a half.

It was something of a wrench to discover, as a result of the peace treaty of 1809, that they were now included in the Russian empire. Their sovereign king, the ruler of Sweden, had sold them down the river to a nation they hated after centuries of brutal struggles. Swedes they were no longer.

At first, Russian rule seemed only slightly different from their previous government. When Finland was incorporated into the empire of Alexander I, it was at a time of political enlightenment. The new republic of American states had been established, and the French had overturned their centuries-old monarchy. Possibly taking warning from these developments, Alexander I treated his new grand duchy not as a conquered province, but as a separate entity. Finland was allowed to retain its constitutional rights, without any change in the laws or their administration. There was still the system of representative government, with the Finnish Diet levying taxes and the Lutheran Church supreme. What was even better, no army service was required.

The czar's policy on Finland was actually a lot more generous than it seems. No other part of the Russian empire was self-governing. For all other provinces of the huge and sprawling nation, the czar was the czar—autocratic and absolute. Only the Finns ran their own show.

In spite of these liberal terms, the Finns did not become Russified. Far from it—they even retained Swedish as their national language. With no conscription, the Finns could now turn wholeheartedly to peaceful pursuits. So they went about their business of beefing up their education programs, codifying their laws, and proclaiming free trade.

It was too good to last.

At least, that's what the czars and their advisors apparently thought as they looked westward at the independent Finns. After all, what right did the Finns have to be treated better than genuine Russians? Considering the way they had fought Sweden's battles against Russia, they weren't entitled to be coddled.

In the closing years of the nineteenth century, a new scheme for handling the grand duchy was concocted when Nicholas II appointed General Nickolai Ivanovich Bobrikoff as his governor in Finland. The reign of tyranny began. No more could Swedish be the official language. Henceforth Russian would be spoken in the schools, in the courts, and in the government. Moreover, the officials would be Russians—all of them. The right of free speech was ignored and the press censored. A network of spies specialized in secret denunciation, bringing about midnight visits and mysterious disappearances, and the right of assembly was abolished. Furthermore, as long as the Finns had fought for Sweden, they were now ordered to fight for Russia.

The Finns were outraged but tried to get relief by peaceful means. Refusing to be conscripted into the Russian army, they paid a ransom of 20 million marks a year. A petition circulated in 1899 was signed by 522,931 people in ten days, but the czar ignored the delegation who presented it and redoubled his autocratic measures.

The pragmatic Finns reasoned that the military might of Russia would mercilessly strangle any attempt at revolution, and their hatred simmered for a time under the surface. Presently they evolved the strategy that has served so well in civil disputes ever since—passive resistance. In spite of reprisals and penalties, Finnish production slackened, and workmanship was inferior. Manufactures arrived in Russia with exasperating slowness, and parts were missing or defective. Finnish soldiers inducted into the armies of Russia were found to be stupid, slow moving, unable to master simple instructions, and totally ineffectual.

The climax came in 1904, when a young patriot who could stand it no longer shot the hated General Bobrikoff. Meeting Bobrikoff on his way to a public function, Eugene Schauman fired three shots at the dictator, who still managed to get to the platform before collapsing, and then killed himself. A letter found in Schauman's pocket explained that he had taken this way of showing Nicholas the gravity of the oppressive situation and of bringing about its correction. He had given his life, he said, as a private citizen, not as a member of any revolutionary group. No one else was to be blamed.

His sacrifice for liberty has not been forgotten. Eugene Schaumann of Porvoo is revered as the man who gave his life in a lone stand against tyranny.

Bobrikoff's assassination scared Nicholas, at least for a time. He made a number of promises, none of which he kept, but at least he did not appoint a substitute for Bobrikoff of the same caliber. Possibly he had his hands full keeping things quiet at home.

The Finns bided their time. Quietly, they prepared for revolution.

All at once trouble erupted in the ulcer spot of Europe, Serbia, with the assassination of the Austrian archduke, Franz Ferdinand. Europe was plunged into World War I.

Russia's participation in the war exposed the corruption of its domestic politics and made it vulnerable. The czar had overreached himself in his own country, too. Now he had a revolution on his hands at home and the demands of fighting a war against Germany and its allies. On November 17, 1917, the Bolsheviks took over the government of Russia.

The Finns saw their chance, and they took it.

Finland proclaimed its independence on December 6, 1917. It had taken almost seven hundred years, but the Finns were free and independent, as they felt they had a right to be.

Even so, it was not a period of halcyon freedom. Russian soldiers, sometimes leaderless, improperly supplied, and lacking in discipline, were overrunning the country. The freedom so suddenly thrust into their hands was strange to them. They used it as license to loot and riot. In Finland, as in Russia, rival governments tried to seize control, with the Socialists or Reds, setting up a government of their own.

The conservative White government of Finland, which was the legally constituted authority, formed an army with Carl Gustav Mannerheim at its head. With arms and supplies from Germany, little by little the Whites took back their country, driving out or subduing the Red Guards, who were backed by the Russian Communists with men and materiel. It was at this time that the friendly feeling for Germany was born. The Finns remember with gratitude that Germany, its back to the wall in battles to salvage a waning power, gave support, and they recall with bitterness the fact that Sweden turned away. No matter that the Germans had started the trouble in the first place. One does not criticize the moral position of the man who holds out his hand to pull you out of quicksand.

A civil war engenders bitterness that smolders, as we know from our own War Between the States, and the long-continued strife in Ireland. Stories of brother against brother, and of neighbor hunting down neighbor cut deep into the fabric of Finnish unity. We cannot begin to assess the suffering.

One ray of sunshine was the generosity of the United States, which offered food and material goods under the guidance of Herbert Hoover. In his task of administering relief to all of Europe in this period of near starvation, Hoover was immeasurably impressed with the determination of the Finns to solve their own problems. "The Finns," he said, "are the most honest of people."

Although the Declaration of Independence of Finland occurred in 1917, for all practical purposes the country was not truly free until a year later, when the last of the Red forces were defeated. After the bitter but little-known struggle, the wounded country gathered itself together and formed a government. Finland became a nation among nations by the Treaty of Dorpat, with boundaries that stretched from the Arctic Ocean to the Gulf of Finland, reaching east from the Gulf of Bothnia, across Karelia almost to what was then Petrograd. It looked like living happily ever after.

Finland's celebrated Ski Troops, stalking Russians during the Winter War of 1939–1940.

CHAPTER 5

THE FINNS ARE FINNS AT LAST

NOW BEGAN a period of intense nationalism given free rein. The war to end all wars was over. Finland, like the rest of the world, was safe for democracy.

The dream lasted twenty-one years.

The events that beset Finland during World War II are chapters of its history that are written in blood. For a few brief, bitter years, the Finns stood alone to prove to the world that their existence as a nation was something they would buy with their lives.

Anyone who lived through those dark times, whatever his or her nationality, can never forget them. First there was the unprovoked attack by Germany on Poland. The Russians, freed by a nonagression pact with Hitler, invaded eastern Poland. France was mobilized. England followed. The German war machine roared through Western Europe. Country after country fell into line on one side or the other.

The Soviet Union demanded that Finland close the Gulf of Finland, give up harbors, and cede land to "prevent invasion of Russia." Russian forces were massed on the Finnish border.

Finland temporized and tried to take a neutral stance. An incident was manufactured that fooled nobody, but it served. Foreign Commissar Molotov said, "Now it's up to the military." In November 1939 the Russians poured over the border and attacked. Such a force is not mobilized

overnight; it was obvious that the earlier diplomatic ne-
gotiations were intended to provide an excuse for the
invasion.

To the horror of the watching world, bombs were
dropped on Finland's defenseless cities. Civilized nations
protested, but the Russians denied the bombing, saying that
they were only dropping food for the poor. The Finns
thereafter referred to Russian bombs as "Molotov bread
baskets."

But it wasn't funny. There were fifty Russian soldiers for
each Finn.

Even so, the Finns' reputation as fearless and staunch
fighters held true. Battered and weary, they held their lines,
and as winter tightened its grip, they attacked. Knowing
what routes the invaders would follow, they caught them
with blistering crossfire in narrow defiles so that the
advance was bottled up and scattered units were vulnerable.
When night came, shadowy forms slipped out of the darkness to pour water over the tank tracks as they parked on
frozen lakes, causing them to freeze to the ice and become
immovable. The world cheered, unbelieving, as the
Russians were forced back by the gallant Finns, who were
fighting what was bound to be a losing battle.

The Finns had two resources: one was the simple, raw
courage of men who would die in defense of their homes,
and the other was their supreme military commander, Carl
Gustav Mannerheim.

Mannerheim was everything a hero should be.

Tall, handsome, and intelligent, this Swede-Finn came
from a baronial family. He began his career in the army of
the czar and became a major-general after a somewhat
inauspicious start. He was dismissed from the Finnish
military academy, which he had entered on his fifteenth
birthday, for going AWOL!

After graduating from the Nikolayev Cavalry School at the top of his class, the dashing young baron began the life of an imperial Russian officer. It was a glittering round of ceremonials and formalities carried out with colorful uniforms, beautiful horses, and the clanking of sabers. Mannerheim even gained a sprinkling of experience in the Russo-Japanese War, during which he discovered the value of discipline. Following that, he spent two adventurous years exploring some little-known parts of Asia whose names have a ring of romance and mystery: Samarkand and the Gobi. He did his work well and was posted to Poland, where he was once again the Chocolate Soldier of musical comedy.

All this ended with the brutal reality of World War I, when the Imperial Army rocked by revolution within its ranks, became an undisciplined rabble. Mannerheim saw his career washed away in the tide of disintegrating authority in which men turned on their officers. It was worth his life to travel in full uniform from Odessa to Helsinki, but that is what he did. When he reached Helsinki, he was given command of Finland's White armies. He was fifty years old.

His military expertise in the bloody civil war turned the tide for the Whites.

The floundering young nation then made a mistake which led to repercussions a quarter of a century later: the Finns accepted help from Germany and turned their backs on the Swedish volunteers who had fought at their side. Mannerheim advised against it but was overruled. Disillusioned and ashamed, he left the country.

When the Finns recovered from their momentary aberration and recalled him, they made him regent until their democratic constitution prevailed and the nation was launched. A year later, Mannerheim was defense minister and watched with growing concern the sinister stirrings in Russia. He urged that the Scandinavian nations join Finland in a mutual defense pact, but nobody listened. Who, they said, wants war? We are peaceable. Who would attack us?

The totalitarian regime next door, that's who.

And so it was that when Germany swamped Norway and Russia bombed Finland, nobody was ready. Mannerheim, who had saved the country twice before, was called upon and under his command the incredible transpired. The nine divisions Finland was able to mobilize held forty-five Soviet divisions at bay for 105 days. The Winter War, as it became known, was an epic battle for survival, in which the Finns took nine Russians for every one of their countrymen.

Finland got a lot of sympathy, but not much else. Neighbor Sweden did what little was done by encouraging young Swedish officers to enlist in Finland's army and sending more than $100 million worth of matériel. The United States contributed a company of Finnish-American volunteers and a loan of $30 million for the purchase of civilian goods. The Western powers agreed to send fifty thousand men, but this offer was nullified when Norway and Sweden would not permit them to cross their borders.

The Soviets made much of the "Mannerheim Line," supposedly a highly fortified defense position, in an attempt to explain their losses. The Mannerheim Line was actually a number of outmoded concrete bunkers with gun tubs, wire, and trenches. The secret of its strength was the Finnish troops.

Mordant humor surfaced.

"Sure, one Finn is worth ten Russians, but what do we do when the eleventh arrives?" Another macabre joke was, "If the Russians keep coming, where will we be able to bury them all?"

What the Finns could not do by desperate resolve, they did by cleverness. A battalion of Russians was deployed to watch a Finnish unit which was a shadow, made largely of cardboard figures and empty tents, with a few living persons to give it substance. Large holes were sawed in the lake ice which the Russians must cross, and their heavy vehicles sank to the bottom. And the Ski Troops, Finland's inspired innovation in modern warfare, could strike like ghosts in their white robes and disappear in a strategy unused since the time of Gustavus Adolphus.

But in the end it was all in vain. Finland had to surrender, and a treaty signed in Moscow on March 13, 1940, made it official.

The Russians' price for peace was a stiff one. They wanted Karelia, the beautiful old cradle of Finnish nationalism. They wanted Petsamo, Finland's outlet to northern waters. They wanted Porkkala, the peninsula so near Helsinki that leasing it for a Russian military base at Hangö was a serious threat to national security. To all of these demands Finland acceded. An uneasy peace followed, and for fifteen months, refugees from the ceded lands began a weary trek to Finnish territory. The exhausted nation began to patch up the wounds of the conflict, resolutely turning away from the factories of Enso Gutzeil, their largest industrial enterprise; their nickel mines; and their Arctic highway, now all in Russian hands.

All at once events in the greater conflict embroiling Europe took an odd turn. Those strange bedfellows, Hitler and Stalin, fell out.

Finland took a desperate chance. Following the annexation of Estonia, Latvia, and Lithuania by the Soviet Union in the summer of 1940, the handwriting on the wall was plain: Finland next. With Germany holding Denmark and Norway, there could be no help from the Allied Nations. The manpower situation in Finland was acute: one out of six people, women as well as men, were under arms. Maintaining a position of absolute neutrality seemed hopeless, and so

Finland gave the Germans permission to move troops across its territory. On June 25, 1941, Russian planes flew over southern Finland, dropping more "Molotov bread baskets." That night Finland declared war on the Soviet Union.

Mannerneim was needed again. He was seventy-four years old and peacefully retired. But there was no one who understood, as he did, both the Germans and the Russians. He was asked to be president and commander-in-chief for life. The old soldier took up his burden and began again to serve his country.

The Continuation War, as it was called, went well at first. Mannerheim's jubilant troops swept across Karelia and reoccupied the province, moving east just far enough to protect the border. There they stayed for two and half years.

So far, it was not technically a war of aggression, but only of liberation. Stubbornly insisting that they were not a part of the larger world conflict, the Finns remained outside Leningrad and refused the German demands that they should attack. This was their own war, they said; they fought it separately from the Germans.

Required by political considerations to support their Russian allies, the British reluctantly asked if Mannerheim planned to invade Soviet territory. Since Mannerheim did not want to betray his plans to Russian ears, he sent an equivocal answer, and the British government, in spite of popular opposition, declared war on Finland.

The United States was under pressure to do likewise, but a strong current of admiration for the sturdy people who paid their debts and took a heroic stand for freedom kept grass roots feeling on the side of Finland. In 1942 the American government urged Finland to make peace.

The Finns replied that they would not fight Americans, even on Finnish soil, but that Americans should not permit their Soviet allies to invade Finland. It was an impasse.

What little military strength Finland had was now exhausted, and the Finns could no longer hold out alone. A Soviet offensive in June 1944 forced them back across Karelia.

So peace came again in much the same form as it had before. Eastern Karelia was lost, this time, the Finns felt, irrevocably. Petsamo and its corridor to the Arctic were given up. The Russians demanded—and got—the right to lease a military base at Hangö. Extortionate reparations were levied.

The most staggering of the Soviet demands in terms of its execution was that the Finns should remove the Germans from their lands.

The Germans would not leave peaceably. They not only refused to withdraw, but they also sent large forces of Storm Troopers to reinforce those already there. As the Finns pushed them toward Norway, they carried out a scorched-earth policy that left the hamlets in their path in smoking ruins. The inoffensive Lapps were the chief victims of their savagery. In Rovaniemi, nine buildings out of ten were destroyed. Kittälä, a city of fifteen hundred, lost every building except the Lutheran Church. With all her other problems, Finland managed to evacuate nearly fifty thousand of Lapland's people. Here, again, Sweden responded generously to the need and gave shelter to the refugees, as many as two thousand a day, who fled the Nazi holocaust.

Refugees also poured into Finland. Eleven percent of the nation's total lands had been ceded, and new homes had to be found for the 12.5 percent of Finland's population who lived there. Of course, said the Soviets, the people could stay if they wished, and become Russians.

There were forty-two thousand Finns living in Karelia. Of this number, the total who elected to remain was nineteen!

And the damages! For defending her sovereignty, Finland had to pay more than $225 million, and this largely in engineering goods and machinery Finland did not produce. Forced to gear up for new industries, Finland built whole plants for Russia with high cost materials under punitive delivery schedules and inspections that seized upon the smallest discrepancy to declare goods valueless. How Finland managed to meet this demand and the others that followed is a story of incredible determination. But Finland did, and what's more, invited the world to visit Helsinki for the Olympic Games in 1952! That's sisu.

Incredibly, the Russians also demanded that the Finnish coat of arms be reversed so that the lion of Finland, brandishing his sword, would face west instead of east. Apparently, they felt threatened by his stance in his age-old position.

The Finns did not take time to weep and mourn. In eight years they paid reparations equal to 80 percent of their peacetime exports, mostly metallurgical products: eighty turbogenerators, seven hundred locomotives, fifty thousand motors and engines, thirty-five thousand tons of cable, and six hundred ships. No other country achieved this; no other country even attempted it.

It wasn't long before the leaders of the United States began to see the error of turning a blind eye toward the dictates of the Soviet Union, but by then it was too late. By Russian terms, Finland still cannot join any alliance.

Even so, our growing respect and admiration for a nation so honest and honorable has led to an unusual situation. Like other countries in Europe, Finland had a war debt to the United States dating from World War I, not for weapons, but for food. As the world geared itself up for World War II, other nations repudiated their debt. But not Finland. Every year Finland paid its obligation, right up until 1949. About that time we recognized the ridiculous position we were in, accepting money from one people only in return for what we had given, while with the other hand we doled out large sums, even to our former enemies, to aid recovery. Why, we wondered, does Finland continue to make these payments?

The answer, said the Finns, was simple: "We owe the money."

The upshot of it was that the money Finland still continues to pay has been channeled into a scholarship exchange system, by which Finnish young people may spend some time in the United States, in the hope that bonds of friendship between the two countries may be strengthened. So far, it's working. Each year, eager, interested young Finnish men and women live and work among us.

And what of Mannerheim?

He remained at the helm until 1946, when he retired. The old warrior was tired and lived only five more years. When his body was returned to Finland after his death in Switzerland, he lay in state for three days as Finns of all ages filed past his coffin in a soundless, grieving procession.

There is much more we could say of Mannerheim, and all of it good. To Finns he is George Washington, Abraham Lincoln, and Winston Churchill rolled into one. He sacrificed everything, time and again, to respond to the call whenever Finland needed him. It would not be hard to believe that if Finland needs him again, like the legendary Väinämöinen, he will be there.

The Finns do not nurse their painful memories. They live without rancor in the shadow of the Soviet Union in an amicable working arrangement. They look to the future, and we, too, should put behind us any muttering over this chapter of Finland's history. In the words of Patrick O'Donovan, "Few countries have been so tricked, betrayed, bullied, sold, deserted, exploited, in modern times. And none have so wonderfully survived it all."

A statue of Czar Alexander II stands before the cathedral in Helsinki's Senate Square.

CHAPTER 6

THE FRAMEWORK OF FREEDOM

IF GOVERNMENT of the people, by the people, and for the people is the ideal, then Finland has it. It is said that there are forty-three countries in the world where the people live in freedom, and Finland is one of them. The Finns, like their neighbors in Norway and Sweden, enjoy the full political rights of a self-governing people, with the right to wrangle about elections and grouse about taxes.

It was not ever thus. When Harald Fairhair enjoyed the revenues of Finland, his tax collector Thorolf was received as joyfully as the plague. Thorolf mourned that while formerly thirty men could manage to separate the Finns from their money, he had to take ninety helpers. But things went smoothly, he said, and relations were friendly for the most part, though occasionally they did have to use force to convince an unregenerate taxpayer. Even in ninth century Finland, the natives resented outside control.

As you recall, the first formal government of Finland was dealt out by the Swedes, who were masters of Finland as early as the thirteenth century. Previous to that there must have been government on the tribal level at least, though there was no written code of laws for many centuries. Since evidence points to Finland's being occupied as long ago as 8000 B.C., we can assume some kind of organization. Authority was the strong-arm kind, and it wasn't handed down. There were no judges or police—if you had trouble with a neighbor, you cracked his skull yourself.

Even under the Swedes, the Finns were self-governing. Oh, there was a governor appointed from Sweden to assure loyalty to the crown. If the Finns were lucky, he might be a truly enlightened, far-seeing administrator such as Count Per Brahe, who built roads and bridges and founded Turku University. He was appreciated, too, since there weren't too many like him.

The Swedish monarchs allowed the Finns a surprising amount of political autonomy, much more than was customary for a conquered province in that day. They had their own representatives and were allowed to make laws that applied to their internal affairs. They furnished soldiers for the never-ending wars of the period and, of course, paid taxes. In return Finland had the flattering status of a "dukedom." Possibly the common people didn't even know they had the empty honor of having the Swedish king's heir known as the "duke of Finland," but at least it was a gesture of respect and some salve to their feelings.

Almost six hundred years of government by Sweden undeniably left its mark on Finnish law and government. Although Russian domination lasted for scarcely more than a century, the Finns stubbornly resisted any attempt to graft Russian customs onto their way of living. In spite of the efforts of Bobrikoff and his ilk, the Finns were determined to retain their institutions, and they did so by whatever means a subject nation may employ: subterfuge, defiance, and slow compliance. When at long last the opportunity presented itself, they threw off the Russian yoke and declared themselves to be what they had always felt they were—free men and women, and Finns.

But they must have felt, even then, that the stable monarchies of Norway and Sweden had something worth emulating. The first thing they did, in setting up a new government, was to invite a foreigner to be king. He was none other than Prince Friederich Karl of Hesse, the brother-in-law of Kaiser Wilhelm II of Germany.

The Finns would like to forget this aberration. Fortunately for them, after Prince Karl studied the situation and even studied the Finnish language (which may have helped discourage him), he regretfully declined. So the Finnish government was set up along the lines of the neighboring Scandinavian states, but the element of monarchy was left out. The Finns seem quite happy with the way it all turned out.

As provided by the constitution, the president is Finland's head of state. This official is elected for a six-year term, and theoretically, at least, upon election the president is nonpartisan. His main functions are to conduct foreign policy, negotiate with other governments, and to form a cabinet. In addition he may initiate and veto legislation although a presidential veto can be overridden by a two-thirds vote of parliament. He has the right to dissolve parliament and to appoint high government officials. He is also the supreme commander of the armed forces.

Since there is no vice-president, there is no one waiting in the wings to take over the president's job. If he is incompetent for some reason, the Finns just elect another one.

The honor of being the first president belongs to Kaarlo Juho Stählberg. Since he is also credited with writing the Finnish constitution, he was probably the best possible choice to interpret it.

The man who holds Finland's highest office has always been one of its most respected citizens. This doesn't mean that there is no contest in the election—far from it!—but the office is sought by individuals of proved statesmanship. It is unheard-of for a dark horse, a person almost unknown, to be chosen, as has happened in our own democracy. Once in office, the president discards party loyalties and puts the interests of the country first.

A dramatic example of this was furnished by the president whose bitter responsibility it was to sign the treaty with Russia that ended the Winter War. President Kyösti Kallio exclaimed, as he signed unwillingly, "Let the hand wither that signs this monstrous document!" To the horror of those who knew of this event, within a year his arm was paralyzed.

Other presidents served so unselfishly that they are revered throughout Finland: Risto Ryti, who guided his country through the alliance with Germany; Carl Mannerheim, the brilliant statesman-general who ranks with the great leaders of the world; Pääsikivi, and Fagerholm. The reason their names are not household words to us is that we are so little acquainted with Finnish politics, for their statesmanship has kept the frail ship of state from foundering on the rocks of Communism.

Once elected, the president has six years to prove that his policies are best for Finland. If they're not, on February 15 the electorate turns out to turn *him* out. And the electorate means every adult. Finnish women have had the vote since 1906, and thus were the first women in Europe to gain this basic democratic right.

Finland's present head of state is Urho Kekkonen, a man whose political career began in 1936. President since 1956, he has proved himself an expert in walking the tightrope of preserving Finnish independence while keeping peace with the neighbor to the east. The Finns aren't bitter, and they have amicable dealings with the Soviet Union, but the president's role is no job for a bull in a china shop. All presidents have walked warily and avoided provocative attitudes. They are aware that theirs is the only nation touching Russia that has not been swallowed up, in spite of the eight-hundred mile border they share.

Kekkonen is very sports minded. As an Olympic high-jump champion, he has been trained physically and mentally to develop stamina. He seems to be in no hurry, and so he is not stampeded by events. Detractors frequently label him an extremist and claim that he promotes Russian detente, even though he opposed concessions right after the war. They mutter that Finland is becoming "Kekkoslovakia."

Those who look at his role from the outside have a different view. According to one Danish observer, "There is hardly any other non-Communist statesman who must steer his ship along a narrower path than the one Finland now has to navigate. Yet in all these years Finland has kept clear of the rocks on which so many political shipwrecks have occurred."

Whatever his political persuasion, the president must form a cabinet that will be acceptable to the parliament. He chooses at least eleven, or as many as sixteen, ministers who conduct the business of government. The prime minister is the senior member of the cabinet and represents it before the parliament. In the president's absence, he or she also performs the presidential tasks.

The Eduskunta is the representative body of Finland. It is a one-house parliament with two hundred members, each elected for a term of four years. The Eduskunta makes the laws, but they are not official unless the president signs them. Representation is proportional to population as in the U.S. House of Representatives. Since there are eight political parties, it is somewhat like a game of musical chairs, especially with regard to the cabinet. If the Eduskunta shows a vote of no confidence in the governing body of ministers the president has selected, it is up to him to nominate a new slate.

The names of the political parties are so similar it is difficult for an outsider to see what differing philosophies they stand for. Oddly enough, there is a powerful Communist party which, of course, calls itself something else. This group was outlawed in 1930, but due to Russian insistence it is now protected by treaty and enjoys the sponsorship of Moscow. It is estimated that one fifth of the voters have Communist leanings.

There is one distinctive feature in Finland's government that we should especially note. That is the official ombudsman, whose unwieldy title is *eduskunnan oikeusasiamies* and whose task it is to receive and report grievances against the government. Finland was the second country in the world to create such an official. More than likely the Finns knew the value of a special people's advocate, as a result of having been governed oppressively.

Whether because of noble examples or because the country is small enough so that iniquity is hard to hide, there is very little corruption in Finnish government. Mannerheim set up the ideal of service to one's country as the honorable Finn's goal, and national pride just doesn't leave room for greedy officeholders.

In its effects on ordinary citizens, Finnish law seems somewhat paternal. The penal code allows no capital punishment. There are work camps for first offenders with emphasis on paying one's debt to society by doing labor that will benefit all. Finns claim that the Helsinki airport was built by drunken drivers, and it is not unknown for some government officials to be seen with shovels in hand, working out their sentences upon conviction for driving while "under the influence." The law is no respecter of persons, with none of our "congressional immunity."

Finland adopted a money system that's fairly easy for the visitor to cope with: the smallest unit is the *penniä*. One hundred penniä make a *markka* (*mk.*), which is sometimes expressed as a *finmark* (*fmk.*).

Like everyone else, the Finns suffer from inflation and complain about taxes. There is some justice in this. Finland has a strong social welfare program, and it takes a large tax bite to support it. Some say the taxes are so prohibitive that if you buy a car for yourself, you are paying for one for the government at the same time in sales tax.

"Scandinavian" is almost a synonym for "socialized," and the welfare state has a firm foothold in Finland. Social security and medical insurance are of long standing. Day care for working mothers and others has been provided for decades. The *puisto-täti*, or "park auntie," a woman who cares for the children at play in city parks is a social institution. Child care is a necessary service, for large numbers of Finnish women are employed professionally, many of them as doctors or dentists.

Public assistance as we know it is unheard of. Instead, all welfare is handled locally and, what's more important, funded locally. Thus compassionate neighbors rather than social workers laboring under a heavy case load deal with those in need, and with the problem better understood, there's a better chance of the right help being given. This system has the added advantage of being better controlled than a national one, and there is less room for cheating.

Local government is divided into twelve provinces, each of which has an elected governor. Provinces are subdivided into 47 towns, 28 boroughs, and 462 rural communes (communities), which are governed by elected councils and which collect taxes to support local institutions. Larger communities have a city manager (*kaupunginjohtaja*) who keeps tabs on local affairs.

Almost every commune has its own hospital, which is known as a "health house." Rheumatic diseases are common in Finland since aching bones and creaking joints are part of the price of a moist climate. Finns try to keep their hospitals cheerful and friendly. The charming "Children's Castle" in Helsinki looks more like a fun house than a hospital.

The state also owns and runs the telegraph, railroad, and the liquor monopoly. Along with the postal service, they ought to supply enough complaints to keep the ombudsman busy!

We don't think of Finland as a country with a war machine and a large standing army, and neither do the Finns. They are aware that without a means of defense, however, it would be impossible to prevent Finland's being exploited or swallowed up by stronger powers. Naturally, then, there is conscription. Finnish men are drafted for military training at the age of twenty so that there is a force to be mobilized in case of emergency. The standing army numbers only seventy thousand, but the reserve force is ten times larger. Finland has cooperated with the United Nations in sending troops to trouble spots such as Korea and Cyprus when needed.

Women do their part. All the Scandinavian countries have recognized the equality of women in terms of employment and political participation. Women in Nordic lands have traditionally held control of their own inheritance. A woman didn't even take her husband's name until the eighteenth century, and then she certainly wasn't subject to him.

Earlier, a woman remained a member of her father's family. A Swede Finn, for instance, might be known as Hulda Martinsdatter, while a Finn-Finn might have the name Priita Maria Sakarintutturi (Bertha Mary, Zachary's daughter). In both cases only their children took the husband's name. This tradition is one reason that the women of Scandinavian lands had an impressive head start while women struggled for their rights and universal suffrage in other parts of the world.

It is no wonder that Finnish women, almost without exception, have careers outside the home. They are especially to be found in the professions, where skill rather than strength is the requisite for success, and some women have reached the highest positions. The professor of criminal law at Helsinki University, the head of Finnish Interpol, and the assistant secretary general in the United Nations Secretariat are all women. Müna Sillanpää was the first woman to be chosen prime minister of Finland.

For a fledgling state, Finland has certainly coped with some formidable problems. The nation has been defeated in war but not occupied and is now the most democratic and prosperous nation that borders Russia. By Russian command Finland cannot ally itself with the West, but it is not a Soviet satellite, either.

Cheerfully fatalistic but not pessimistic, the Finns go on, minding their business. Making the most of the art of the possible is their only weapon, so let us hope that this is enough to keep them free.

Akseli Gallen-Kallela took inspiration from the *Kalevala*, Finland's folk epic. Here the artist depicts the witch Louhi attacking Väinämöinen and his faithful followers.

CHAPTER 7

FINLAND'S NATIONAL SCRAPBOOK

A STUDENT at Turku University in 1547 who went into a bookstore and asked for a book in Finnish would have been hooted out of the place. There weren't any.

Not that Finnish was not spoken at the time—it was the language the common people knew—but Finnish was not the language of the educated, and there was no written alphabet. If you were Finnish and wrote anything at all, it had to be in some other tongue.

It was not until 1548 that Michael Agricola, a bishop of Turku who had been a pupil of Martin Luther and Philip Melanchton, published the first Finnish alphabet book. He followed this up with a translation of the New Testament. Thus there was finally a book in the Finnish language, sixty-three years before the King James Bible was completed in England. There was a long time lapse, however, until the first Finnish-Latin dictionary followed in 1826. (Even then, those two-inch words must have given the lexicographers trouble!) Now, at last, there could be Finnish literature.

All this was helped along by a professor, Henrik Gabriel Porthan, a man of many talents. Although history was his subject, he published the first Finnish grammar and, in 1788, a collection of Finnish folklore that was not in Finnish. Known now as the Father of Finnish History, he tried to instill in his students a desire to know more about their heritage and urged them to look for it in their nation's folklore.

There were other leaders with the same goal. Johan V. Snellman kept harping, "One language, one nation." Johan Ludwig Runeberg came out with a book of tales about heroic Finns at war with (who else?) Russians. Finnish shirt buttons began to pop when Sir Edmund Gosse wrote that a notable part of Sweden's glories had been contributed by Finns, even in literature. But it was a bitter pill that it was Swedish literature, and the Finns listened more and more to Runeberg's exhortation: "Without the Finnish language, we are not Finns!"

Now comes Elias Lönnrot upon the scene.

How Lönnrot ever managed to get to college is a marvel. He was the middle child of a destitute family sustained by bread made of pine bark and soup of lichens. The father, a tailor, evidently decided that life was hopeless and took refuge in the bottle. As was the custom, his sons attempted to follow his trade when they weren't eking out a little extra by begging. Elias was a dreamer and a reader, and of so little practical use that his older brother finally said, "He'll never make it as a tailor; let him study." Elias did so and attended the University of Turku where he qualified as a physician.

Caught up with other scholars in the nineteenth-century wave of nationalism, Lönnrot burned with a desire to rescue the heritage of Finland from oblivion. He began to take note of the runes he heard in the outlying provinces. These runes were legends, charms, proverbs, and poems sung or chanted to one melody and in one meter. At first, Lönnrot was a bit handicapped in that he heard the runes in Finnish but all he could write in was Swedish. The ancient runes so intrigued him that he learned to write in his native language without, one might add, a grant from a foundation.

As he worked, he began to realize that the same song

appeared in different areas, but that the older ones seemed to come from Karelia. He also observed that the legends could be strung together to make a story, somewhat in the manner of the separate tales of the *Odyssey* forming a complete whole.

The tales had been preserved and recited for special occasions by rune singers in remote villages. In backwoods homes Lönnrot would find old men, and sometimes old women, who would perform for him. He discovered that occasionally he had better results by offering a little lubrication for their tonsils, in which case they might sing all night. Touchingly grateful at being recognized, they would sing their entire repertoire, a fascinating outpouring of ballads, peasant lore, and advice for living. The runes were a collection in song of the myriad things that a latter-day person might clip and paste into a scrapbook, but they had been preserved for posterity through generations of rune singers, who had stored them only in their memories.

There was a definite ritual. The lead singer and his second would sit side by side on a bench or face each other on parallel benches. An accompanist with the *kantele*, a Finnish harp, would sit to one side, and the singing would begin. The lead singer would sing a line, such as

He struck his steed with his whip.

The second, when he recognized it, would join in, so that the last foot of the line was sung by both. Then he would embellish it with a refrain that echoed the thought:

. . . made a ringing sound with the beaded lash.

They would continue:

The spirited steed started to run fast,
. . . the horse to trot along.

> The horse ran one verst, a second;
> . . . the best of horses in the land flew along a bit.
> Then it came to a sudden stop,
> . . . does not stir from the spot.

The lives of these people were pitifully meager (Lönnrot said that the only food he saw was bread, fish, and clabbered milk), but Lönnrot was so entranced with their poetry that he made eleven trips in all, over the length and breadth of Finland. There were difficulties. During an epidemic he once found thirty-five sick people in one room, and he visited hamlets where one out of every six or seven died. Sometimes the old people were afraid. There had been attempts to eradicate the old beliefs as being un-Christian. In one village where Lönnrot had been collecting material, the church was struck by lightning, and the event was regarded as evidence of the wrath of the Almighty at such ungodly goings-on. The singers got religion on the spot and refused to sing another note.

When Lönnrot published the *Kalevala* in 1835, it was a wellspring of Finnish national pride. Finland now had a folk epic, a colorful fabric of legends woven by countless elders through the ages.

Unlike Homer's epics and the Arthurian legends, the *Kalevala* tales are not of gods and goddesses or kings and knights. Their heroes are not even heroes in the usual sense since the heroic Finns vanquished their enemies not by feats of derring-do, but by powerful words and magical sayings.

Chief among them was Väinämöinen, who dallied around in his mother's womb for thirty summers and winters and was seven hundred years old when he was born. (Explain that, if you can.) He was the hero-leader, resourceful and bold, who brought trees and flowers to the barren rock shield of Finland. "Old and steadfast," he is called over and over, and he had a long beard that was the chief reason for his unsuccessful wooing.

In spite of his age and wisdom, Väinämöinen was certainly foolish over women. On a trip to Lapland he met the beautiful daughter of the witch Louhi and tried to impress her with a few samples of his magic. He peeled a stone the way you would an onion and then ate it, tied an egg in a knot, and made a pole out of a piece of ice. She was not impressed. She wanted a *sampo*, a mechanical marvel of Finnish ingenuity that would grind corn on one side, household articles on another side, and money out of a third. This was not Väinämöinen's specialty, but it seemed like the sort of thing his partner, Ilmarinen, could handle. Building a sampo would be a simple job for the clever blacksmith who had forged the heavens.

By singing up a golden tree, Väinämöinen bamboozled Ilmarinen into climbing it. Then he sang up a big wind and had his friend blown to Lapland. Trusty Ilmarinen made the sampo and thus became the promised bridegroom of Louhi's daughter, no doubt because he was younger and handsomer than Väinämöinen.

The more he thought about it, the more Väinämöinen wanted that sampo. He mounted an expedition and persuaded Ilmarinen, among others, to help him steal the prize from the smithy's future mother-in-law.

Their boat got stuck on the back of a large pike, a predicament which could have been a disaster, but being resourceful Finns, they ate him for several days. After that, Väinämöinen made a harp from the pike's jaw. Then, as the Frank Sinatra of his day, he entertained his crew with songs so sad that their tears ran into the sea, where they became pearls, and the men became music lovers, and Väinämöinen was established as a poet.

They were successful in stealing the sampo, but a great

battle followed, in which Väinämöinen and Louhi hurled magic spells at each other instead of spears. In the final struggle both wizards were clutching the sampo as they fell into the sea. Väinämöinen, however, was the ultimate victor: he gathered up some pieces of it which he planted, and up they came!

Louhi didn't give up easily; she then stole the sun and the moon. Väinämöinen found them chained to rocks inside a hill in Lapland. Here for once Väinämöinen used his sword and lopped off the heads of the three Lapps guarding the celestial prisoners. (The fact that his sword was one barleycorn longer than theirs gave him first whack, according to the rules.) Then he set Ilmarinen to making tools so that he might free them. Louhi got the idea that Ilmarinen was forging a neck ring to chain her and released the sun and moon herself.

Next she tried to exterminate Väinämöinen's people, the clan of Kaleva, with diseases furnished to her by Ukko, chief of the gods. But Väinämöinen won that round, too, being a better prayer. Ukko was so entranced with his poetry that he gathered all the diseases together, and they were washed away in the bathhouse.

It's worth noting that Väinämöinen did all this with words, for they are the beginning and end of Finnish magic. No black cats at midnight, no wishbones, no lamps to rub, no pins in dolls. Just words. But they must be the right ones.

And songs. According to the bards of the *Kalevala*, Väinämöinen was the greatest of singers.

> Never have I heard such music
> As was played by Väinämöinen
> Joyous and primeval minstrel.

The poems that concern the smith, Ilmarinen, tend to be almost comic. It is as if the Finns see in him their own natural proclivities. They delight in poking sly fun at his propensity for being led into trouble by others, his ability to make anything at all, and his unquestioning loyalty to his own that compels him to join in their projects whatever the cost to himself.

The beautiful daughter of Louhi whom, you will remember, Ilmarinen had won by doing a favor for Väinämöinen, turned out to be a disagreeable, malicious shrew. Nevertheless, Ilmarinen mourned for her when she met a violent end at the hands of a fellow Finn. In looking for a replacement, he was mindful that it would be possible to make improvements in the design, so this time he built his wife out of precious metals, and the effort of creating her nearly melted the neighborhood. Beautiful as she was, she was not quite what one would want as a bedfellow on cold nights. After a night of enjoying her company, in which he froze his arm in spite of being covered with five blankets, three bearskins, and six woolen coats, Ilmarinen offered her, sight unseen, to Väinämöinen.

Väinämöinen was always looking for a wife without much success. He said that he'd take anything good-looking, character being of no consequence. Ilmarinen pointed out hopefully that this woman wouldn't be overly talkative, wouldn't slander his relatives, and wouldn't take more than her share of the bed. He also offered to file down her chin or make other small changes. Väinämöinen was tempted but on seeing her, he had the good sense to decline, saying that it isn't wise to have more gold than one needs. He suggested giving her to the Russians, who, being greedy, would fight over her and destroy themselves.

Ilmarinen couldn't bring himself to give her to the Russians (whom he knew he hated, though he had never met one), or to melt her down. He finally dropped her into the lake.

He then repeated his first mistake of going to Lapland for
another daughter of Louhi. He was by no means welcome,
but Ilmarinen didn't suffer from false modesty. Thinking
the girl couldn't possibly refuse such a good catch, he
abducted her.

She turned out to be a real treasure, both beautiful and
hardworking. But she complained endlessly, even comparing
him unfavorably to the smelly animals. Equal rights being a
thing of the future, Ilmarinen solved his problems by singing
her into a seagull so that she could scream to her heart's
content. After that he gave up romance.

Although Väinämöinen is the central character, it is Ilmarinen who is the most consistently Finnish in his straightforward honesty, his acceptance of others at their own
valuation, his wry humor, and his ability to make what was
never made before.

The reckless, adventurous Lemminkäinen is the Finnish
counterpart of Don Juan. Never believing for an instant
that anyone could resist him, Lemminkäinen also went to
Lapland in search of a wife. He kidnapped Kylikki and stole
her father's bearskin at the same time. In spite of her misgiv-
ings at Lemminkäinen's wretched hovel and scrawny cattle,
she turned out to be a model wife. She didn't even seem to
mind it when he started staying out all night, perhaps
because she was up to a little fun of her own. Then Lemminkäinen's troublemaking sister revealed that Kylikki went
out dancing while he was away. Another romance down the
drain.

The Lappish boy, Joukahainen, shared with the other
male characters a complete inability to see himself objective-
ly. His hang-up was that he thought of himself as a greater
poet than Väinämöinen. The old bard tried to be patient,
but Joukahainen grew unbearably arrogant, and finally
Väinämöinen was angry.

Magic songs, he stormed, are not children's songs or women's jokes. He sang Joukahainen's sleigh into logs in a pond, and his horse into a rock. The now-frightened youth he sang into a swamp up to his chin. In desperation Joukahainen offered anything he could think of for his release and finally hit on the right bribe—his lovely sister.

The anguish of Aino, sold into marriage by her brother and forced to go through with it by her mother, is briefly told. She had to obey her mother, but she was heartsick. Old, bearded Väinämöinen was repugnant to her. Even the thought that she would wear the golden bridal veils of the daughters of the sun and moon could not console her. She put them on as she went to her death in the lake.

If there's anyone who resembles a Greek hero in the *Kalevala,* it is brooding, sullen Kullervo. He lived only to avenge his father's death at the hands of a rival clan.

Weak-witted but immensely strong, Kullervo broke his own cradle when he was just three days old. His enemies were aware that it would be dangerous to let him grow up, so they did everything they could to exterminate him. They tried drowning, hanging, and burning, but nothing worked. Then they farmed him out as a servant, but he was so unteachable that he was sold to Ilmarinen in exchange for a pile of junk iron. Ilmarinen was not too happy with the bargain.

Kullervo could do a little magic, too, and when Ilmarinen's shrewish wife served him a stone for lunch, his temper got the best of him and he had her torn to bits by bears. Grim fate followed him. He unknowingly seduced his own sister, and she took her life. He wiped out the enemy clan, and his own family was destroyed as well. Alienated from the world, he asked his sword to kill him. "I have shed innocent blood, why not the guilty?" it replied. And so ended his joyless existence. There is a moral added to this tale: If you rock your child too much in his cradle, you may addle his brains.

The final scenes of the epic bring us into the Christian era. Marjatta, a pregnant virgin of spotless purity, was forced to bear her child in the squalid sauna of an outlander. Then, over Väinämöinen's protests, Marjatta's son was christened king of Karelia. The old wizard, disgruntled and petulant, sang his last song and went away, leaving his harp behind for the people of Finland. He is presumably still out there on the airwaves, ready to return when Finland needs him.

Interspersed in the narrative fabric of the *Kalevala* are bits and pieces that show the daily life of the Finnish peasant: long descriptions that vividly picture homes, the paraphernalia of work, and closeness to nature. Animism is obvious. There are charms to calm snakes, control bears and cattle, and hunt game animals. As a matter of fact, there are more than sixty charms given, so if you have been hankering to do a little magic like stanching blood, expelling water dragons, or warding off wolves, there's a recipe in the *Kalevala*. You can also find advice for girls on how to be beautiful:

> For one year eat sweet butter; you will get plumper than others.
> For a second year eat pork; you will get handsomer than others.
> For a third year eat cream cakes; you will get to be lovelier than others.

You will also gain so much weight, you will be unable to leave your chair!

Women come in for quite a bit of instruction. The bride-to-be is exhorted to get up before dawn, carry wood, grind grain, knead bread, wash the baby (not hers, his sister's), count the spoons in case the dog may have dragged one off, tote water, heat the sauna, never gossip, bow low to his parents, and do everything in a hurry lest they think her lazy. After all this effort, she should not expect her in-laws to like her:

> Soon, you will experience, unhappy girl,
> to experience, you of hard lot,
> The father-in-law's bony jaw,
> the mother-in-law's stony tongue,
> The brother-in-law's cold words,
> the tosses of the sister-in-law's head. . . .

> A maiden in her father's house
> is like a berry in a garden,
> But a daughter-in-law
> like a dog in chains is bound.
> Seldom does a slave get love,
> a daughter-in-law never.

It is definitely a man's world. While the poor bride gets 850 lines of instruction, the groom gets by with only 264, and precious little of that related to any responsibilities he has in the household. No wonder most of the girls in the *Kalevala* had to be kidnapped!

Here and there are poems that deal with the activities of the ancient Finns, such as bear hunting. (The bear is called by names such as "Honey-paws," and impromptu songs are sung at the feast in which he is the main dish, honoring his prowess.) The few martial pursuits that are described appear in the constant skirmishes between the men of Kaleva and the tribes of Pohjola. War, however, is not looked upon as glorious. One poem bewails the fate of the unlucky youth conscripted into the army where, after a haircut, he will be shoved into boots and a uniform, handed a sword, and then hauled off to maneuvers. (The draft wasn't much different even then!)

The religious background is pagan. Ukko, Ahti, and Tapio are the deities controlling life, water, and forest. Everything has a soul, or perhaps we should call it a spirit. The heroes are not gods, but wizards. They are earthy, artless, lovable, and three dimensional, and their stories are delightful and whimsical.

The *Kalevala* legends have contributed much to Finnish art. Sibelius based most of his symphonic poems on them, and he is by no means the only one who mined their riches. There are ten musical works by Finnish composers on Kullervo alone, including an opera. The *Kalevala* has also inspired sculptors and painters, notably Akseli Gallen-Kallela, whose powerful canvasses have an emotional intensity that brings out the intrinsic dignity of the heroes. Their works express a feeling of sacred trust in their portrayals of Väinämöinen as a Moses-like leader or a Titan aided by cohorts who are real and sincere in their struggles against diabolical forces.

Not only Finland has felt the impact of the *Kalevala*. Longfellow was so impressed that he copied the meter (trochaic tetrameter, if you want to be technical) for *Hiawatha*, which was published in 1855. Perhaps he admired it enough to use it for his model because he sensed a similarity between two struggling, valiant peoples whose age-old legends were safeguarded by their elders.

The *Kalevala's* importance to Finland is not easily stated. It fostered a sense of history, a pride in tradition, and a new awareness of national unity. It was also seen as a work of surpassing beauty. A national treasure, which brought to light the all-but-forgotten symbolic history of the nation, had been restored.

There came a time when the modest Lönnrot was suspected of having done more than just string other people's runes together in a loosely constructed narrative. Possibly because of MacPherson's *Ossian*, which had been hailed as a masterpiece resurrected from ancient manuscripts and later exposed as the work of a modern genius, Lönnrot's work came under closer scrutiny. Some scholars now feel that there is reason to believe he quite frequently improved on the chants as the old men sang them. If he did, it must still be considered a work of love and stunning devotion.

There were other students, urged by Porthan, who also went about collecting folk tales. Nevertheless the credit for rescuing Finland's national scrapbook belongs to Lönnrot. Although Porthan pointed the way and Karl Akseli Gottlund suggested a plan for linking the poems in 1817, it was Lönnrot who brought it all about.

A boy and his reindeer.

CHAPTER 8

THE DISPOSSESSED

THERE IS A PART OF FINLAND that is a forgotten corner of the world, where time is unimportant, and a few people still follow the ways of their ancestors. The hostile environment of Lapland has made it the last wilderness of Europe, and even that is yielding to the press of civilization.

Where the Lapps came from is anybody's guess. For want of a better explanation, scholars concede that they were in Finland when the first "Finns" (whoever they were) hove upon the scene. The Lapps must have been the sort of people they are now—generous, gentle, and unworldly—for they uncomplainingly gave up their homeland and moved farther north. Any bitterness they may have felt lies hidden in their name for themselves: Samek or Sabmelazzak means "the banished" or "the dispossessed."

A Lapp writer, Johan Turi, claims that the Lapps were not only the first people in the area, but also that they had always been there. Neither were there any other people living in the territory. If this is true, then the stone implements which archeologists have found and dated as being more than eight thousand years old must have been the work of Lapps. In any case, if they were not the work of Lapps, whose were they?

As a people, the Lapps have never been very numerous. Like the Eskimos, they are a small people with small families, but they bear no close resemblance to any other group.

Black haired and black eyed, with tawny skin, they are short in stature and slight in build. Very few Lapp men are taller than five feet, and the women are even shorter.

Presently there are perhaps twenty-five hundred Lapps in Finland. This estimate is a little complicated by the existence of a part-Lapp population. Are they Lapps or are they Finns? How much Lapp blood entitles you to be considered a Lapp and vice versa? The number of true Lapps is much smaller than the mixed-blood people. They have a language of their own, which they share with Swedish and Norwegian Lapps. None of these people speaks the language of their governing nation as a first language.

Their land is a land where winter reigns supreme. It begins in early October and becomes progressively colder and darker. Snow lies on the ground to a depth of two feet much of the time and ice grips the waters for nearly eight months, although temperatures average near the zero mark. This is considerably warmer than the range of temperatures to be encountered in Alaska and Canada, and naturally there is more vegetation. There are fifty-one days of continuous darkness in Lapland.

People of earlier times and other nationalities looked upon the Finns as sorcerers, but the Finns in their turn considered the Lapps to be wizards with a hotline direct to the demons. A Lapp could curdle milk or give you smallpox just by thinking about it. If he chanced to look at you as he was passing by, your days were numbered. Since Lapps could supposedly control the forces of nature, understand the speech of animals, and see through walls, their neighbors had a healthy fear of them. Finns might be capable of a little rough magic, but the Lapps had the power of the Evil Eye.

Perhaps one reason that other nations have historically lumped the Finns and Lapps together is that their languages are related. This is not to say that they are similar. Both peoples have a Finno-Ugrian language, but Finns and Lapps each speaking their own tongue will not be able to communicate. For that matter, even among the Lapps there are different dialects (Mountain Lapp being the most common in Finland), but most Lapps can understand one another.

Philologists have turned up some interesting facts about the Lapp language. They say that one word out of four refers to reindeer. The Lapp word for reindeer is a term meaning "what one lives on," and there is a separate name for the male reindeer for each year of his age. "Snow" is not just snow, as it is with us. There are hundreds of words for it, each specifying its density, depth, age, condition, and so on. There is the snow that falls in October, snow that is powdery, snow that has an icy crust, yesterday's snow, and a host of intricate distinctions.

A rather poignant characteristic is the very large number of words describing family relationships. Unquestionably family life is important to the Lapps, since so many of them have lived in isolation except for their own little group.

The traditional Lapp way of life resembled that of the Plains Indians of the American past in its dependence on one resource. For the Indians, it was the buffalo. For the Lapps, it was the reindeer.

The animals were there first, living on the browse and moss. Then came the Lapps, but who knows from where, or when? They began by hunting the reindeer as the Indians hunted the buffalo, following the herds as they migrated from summer pasture to winter yard, from grass to lichen. Like the Indians, the Lapps evolved the first mobile home: a tent. Then they went one step farther and began herding the animals that were once their quarry.

The reindeer gave the Lapps their entire economy—their

horses for traveling and drawing loads, their cows for milk
and meat, their sheep for hides and leather, and their decoys
for enticing wild reindeer into their herds. The lack of
adequate pasture, however, made settled homes an impos-
sibility. The reindeer must be herded to where the food was.

The Mountain Lapps subsisted almost entirely on
reindeer as a basic life support, but other Lapps had
additional sources of income. The River Lapps added
fishing as a means of extending their food supply, and the
Forest Lapps trapped furs. Only recently have Lapps turned
to the raising of crops.

As bigger, more aggressive groups of people moved into
their homeland, the Lapps kept to themselves and
withdrew. Farther, and farther, and farther.

There was an attempt, by an edict of 1690, to legislate
integration of Finns and Lapps: they could live in the same
territory, provided they didn't encroach on each other's
means of livelihood. This sounded good, but in practice it
didn't work out so well. The Finns' farms took up land that
was badly needed for reindeer pasture, and the Finns in their
turn weren't very pleased when their crops were eaten by the
Lapps' animals. And the more numerous the Finns became,
the more they whittled away at the few privileges guaranteed
to the Lapps, such as the right to trap beaver.

As if it weren't difficult enough to be a Lapp in such
circumstances as these, more than one nation claimed their
allegiance. Swedish and Norwegian rulers squabbled over
who should be called "King of Lapps," and even Denmark's
kings made a grab at Lapland. Sometimes the Lapps had to
pay taxes to three governments. This certainly shows their
uncomplaining nature.

There was a fourth government that still exists today. It is
an organization of reindeer herders called the *paliskunnat*,
with an elected chairman for each local unit and a

central governing body. Its main function is advisory, much like a cooperative marketing association, and it has some judiciary power. Some Lapps, following the lead of minority groups like the American Indian, are becoming more organized and vocal in their attempts to retain their identity, even to the point of putting up their own candidates for parliament.

The reindeer is not now the backbone of Lapp economy, as it once was. Although the herds are larger, the number of herdsmen has declined. Today, only about 10 percent of Finland's Lapps rely on reindeer as their main source of income.

For those who do, herding customs follow the age-old pattern, with modern overtones. During the summer the reindeer range over the highland pastures. When autumn comes, it is time for the annual roundup. This is a time of celebration. Herders and their families socialize while the owners gather together their own animals, which have been earmarked, and take them to lower-level pastures. There is noise and color and excitement in the roundup, a mixture of work and festivity. Along with the sorting, inoculating, and branding, there is the exuberance of lassoing, antler-wrestling, and reindeer racing. Slaughtering for market takes place in January, in an assembly-line setup, with government inspection a must. This harvest is usually 30 to 35 percent annually, resulting in an impressive income for those who are part of it.

Nowadays only the herdsmen follow the deer. When the herds gather in the southern sector for the winter, their masters have several months of domestic life in their home communities, where Lapp families usually remain throughout the year.

Things have changed in other ways. Though the herds are larger (from five to ten thousand animals), the herdsmen are fewer. They zip over the frozen tundra on snowmobiles, not skis, to tend and round up their charges. Tending the herd is no longer a matter of eagle-eyed watchfulness, since there are binoculars to spot the strays and helicopters to locate the runaways. The skin tent, with its floor of birch branches covered with reindeer hides, is still in evidence.

For the reindeer there is little difference. They still forage for themselves, digging in the snow for the lichens that are their basic winter food. Lapps say that when reindeer are offered moss which someone else has found for them, the animals refuse it. By instinct they locate the moss even under several feet of snow. Nature has provided them with hooves like shovels for scraping away the snow to reach the delectable, life-giving tidbits. The giant herds rove unmolested on the inland tundra, avoiding humans as much as possible.

Outsiders are apt to overlook the demanding aspects of Lapp life, and sigh for the colorful days when the reindeer was the sole sustenance of these hardy, uncomplaining nomads. In times past the Lapps derived all their needs from the reindeer and wasted none of it. Bones were used to make buttons, horns, and decorations and cracked to extract marrow. Blood, mixed with organ meats, suet, and barley meal, was stored in casings like sausage as a preventative for scurvy. Scraps and offal were frozen for dog food, and the reindeer meat itself was the mainstay of the Lapps' diet, along with the native berries and fish.

From the hides came the skins from which gloves, shoes, leggings, and the like were fashioned. Hides also furnished skin coverings for sledges and the baby's cradle. Sinews became thread, and antlers were fashioned into knife handles and trinkets.

Women made the clothing and also cured the meat and chewed the sinews into thread. Men were usually busy enough with the herding.

It didn't leave much time for fun, but the Lapps did invent a musical instrument of their own. It's a small reed pipe, a very appropriate device for a herder. They also have a musical saw, and there's a traditional chant called the *joika,* which sings of sun, storms, snow, reindeer, and the elements of their life that make up the country music of their choice.

The Lapps had no chance to become artists as we think of the term, unless we consider living in tune with nature an art in itself. Of this they were masters, putting color and beauty into the skills needed for living. They did a little weaving and made baskets out of birchbark. They carved and sewed and were skilled craftsmen in all that they did.

It was in their dress, however, that the Lapps really gave vent to their artistic urges. The man wore a knee-length jacket known as a *kufta*, of bright blue wool, embroidered in strong primary colors and trimmed with metal. His trousers were breeches made of reindeer hide, which were worn with fur leggings. On his feet he wore moccasins of reindeer fur with upcurving toes, gaily embroidered, with bright red laces. His long fur coat, called a *pesk*, slipped over his head like an Eskimo parka. He wore it with a belt in which a knife called a *puukko* was tucked. The puukko served as a tool as well as a weapon, and no male Lapp would feel dressed without it.

The woman's dress was almost the same except that her kufta was longer. Only in their headgear was there "separate but equal" styling. The woman's cap was bright red with blue and yellow trimming, while the man wore the traditional "Cap of the Four Winds." It was bright blue and had a point jutting out in each of the four directions, stuffed with feathers. Beautiful!

Today Lapps in traditional costume can be seen driving late model cars up to their frame houses in towns that look much like any other northern outpost. Reindeer are no

longer "what one lives on." Domesticated reindeer now
form a worldwide business. Though families that own them
may still avail themselves of the traditional products, they
are much more likely to market the meat as a gourmet treat
and ship the antlers to the Orient, where they rival ginseng
as a rejuvenator of tired old glands. The money buys
gasoline for the snowmobile.

Romantic as it may seem, herding has problems. They are
not merely the simple ones of runaway herds and stern
demands for brawn and endurance. The free life-style has a
built-in insecurity, for the herder's fortune is running loose
in the fells, prey to foul weather and rapacious wolves. Calf
loss is as high as 50 percent, and sometimes it is total.
Mature reindeer may starve when ice under the snow wipes
out their food supply or may be swept away by an epidemic
of brainworm. Their very survival is threatened by the
specter of overgrazing, and Lapps must now pay an
indemnity to farmers whose crops the reindeer damage.

As the world grows more concerned with ethnic cultures
merging and being forgotten, the countries where the Lapps
live and work are giving much thought to the needs of these
uncomplaining people so that their way of life may survive.
It is a difficult balancing act in which new methods of herd
management and range improvement are balanced against
the traditional social and cultural patterns of the Lapps.

A Lapp child going to an outside school, for instance,
may feel out of step with his own people and never return to
their ways, even though few of them pursue higher education
or become professionals. The obvious need is for vocational
training. According to a law now in effect in Norway, no
Lapp two generations away from herding may resume it,
and the door to the former life-style may soon be closed. Old
ways have inevitably changed, due partly to the influence of
educational television, radio, and several Lappish news-

papers. The latter are distributed free of charge by the Association of Finnish Lapps, organized in 1945, and the Society for the Promotion of Lapp Culture, formed in Helsinki in 1932.

The impact of deforestation, mining, dam building, railroads, and highways has eroded the delicate bond with nature, upset herds, and desecrated sacred places. Tourism, which delights in seeing the Lapp unchanged from the wild free life, has brought in such anachronisms as cabarets and theaters. The thirty thousand inhabitants of Rovaniemi are inundated by four hundred thousand visitors in a year, all eager to see wild reindeer, wild Lapps, and the Hotel Pohjanhovi, which can seat six hundred guests in its dining room.

The Lapps are on their way to extinction. It is even said that as the Lapps continue to drift southward, attracted by easier living, Finnish Lapland will be empty by the year 2000.

There is a paradox in the fact that those who would establish new industries to enable the Lapps to stay as they are ignore the effect of these industries on the environment. Exploiting the mineral wealth will wipe out the wilderness. When that is gone, the reindeer herding, as well as back-up industries like home crafts, fishing, and tourism, will disappear; the true Lapps, their livelihood gone, will disappear also. People from outside Lapland will fill the jobs in industry. The name "Lapp," meaning "nomad," will lose its meaning. The gentle people will be scattered to the four winds their colorful caps immortalize. The dress, homes, and customs molded by their life-style will be the stuff of museums and archives.

Truly ancient churches are rare in Finland since fire was an ever-present danger to the wooden structures. This one in Petäjä dates from 1763.

Chapter 9

THE FLAME OF FAITH

As in most democratic nations of the world, religious tolerance is enjoyed in Finland. You are free to attend services in the church of your choice. You may find it hard to find the church of your choice, however, unless it happens to be Lutheran. At last count 92 percent of all Finns were Lutheran, with a sprinkling of Finnish Orthodox, the next largest denomination, accounting for 1.3 percent. But at that, many other sects were represented, and the number of Quakers had doubled from one to two!

You are free to stay home, too. So many Finns take advantage of this freedom that actual church attendance is about 2 percent, perhaps because the Lutheran church is state supported. To the Finns, the church is a fact of their existence that does not stand or fall by their contributions on Sunday morning. Moreover, it plays an important part in their rites of passage—confirmations, weddings, and funerals—and inattention to regular churchgoing does not reflect a lack of religious feeling.

From time to time a major revival sweeps the country with a new upsurge of religious fervor. Such movements make a lasting imprint on Finnish Lutheranism for, although they have their own emphasis and programs, all have remained within the church. Two of them, the Herännyt ("Awakened") and the Laestadians, draw tens of thousands to their summer mass meetings.

The Finnish people have always believed in a spiritual existence outside themselves. Early Finns followed a shamanistic faith we call animism: a reliance on wizards and a belief that each created thing has a spirit of its own. There was a tree spirit, and a spirit in the water, and a spirit in the air, who for the most part were helpful rather than vengeful or tyrannical. If you wanted something—the right tree for a boat, for instance—you asked for it politely and there was no need for a sacrifice to put a capricious god or goddess in good humor. It was a very comforting religion for people with plenty of difficulties of their own.

They had their own theory of creation, too, which credited Finland with being the first land in all the world. After quite a bit of sloshing around on timeless seas, according to the *Kalevala*, a goldeneye egg divided. The lower half became the earth and the top half, the heavens. The sun was formed out of the top half of the yolk and the moon, from the top half of the white. Where there were mottled spots, these became stars, and any black specks were turned into clouds. (It was not a completely fresh egg, one would think!) After the ten years or so that it took to form the headlands, fish holes, and other features of Finland's island-dotted coast, greater lands and continents followed. After thirty years Väinämöinen made his appearance in the world and, after spending six years being tossed upon the sea, he stepped ashore on the uninhabited, treeless Finnish coast. He arranged with Sampsa, the spirit of arable land, to clothe the barren rock in soil, fields, and trees. That attracted the birds, and the eagle was so grateful to Väinämöinen for fixing up a rest stop for him that he brought the old singer some fire. Things seemed to be finished at that point, except that Ilmarinen claimed the credit for forging the heavens.

Eventually, the world and those governing it grew a bit more sophisticated. Väinämöinen visited several deities

who had more authority than had originally been part of the
act. These were custodians of certain areas of life. There was
Death's blind daughter, for instance, who let loose a horrible array of ailments when she gave birth to nine sons in one
night. She gave them the delightful names of Bellyache,
Gout, Boils, Scabby, Cancer, Plague, Sudden Stitch, and
Rickets and apparently couldn't think of anything equally
attractive for the last one. There were twenty-three deities in
all, including Tapio, who had authority over forests and
gave his name to the city of Tapiola.

The dead gathered for their afterlife in a land which was
reached by crossing a stream, the River of the Dead. Väinämöinen once made the trip to Death's domain, where the
Demon ruled, in order to collect some special recipes he
needed in his pursuit of a reluctant maiden. He found that it
was far from a happy hunting ground, though the Demon
had elk, horses, swans, and presumably other animals as
well. He was a little put off at being served beer in a stoup
containing frogs and snakes along with the brew. When he
got back, he advised against anyone's going there until they
absolutely had to.

All things considered, you could get along pretty well in
life if you knew your *Kalevala*. You simply used whatever
charm was appropriate, whether it was the one for conjuring
up magic ski equipment or brewing beer. If your guests
overstayed their welcome, there were charms for sending
others home and if you preferred a more permanent effect,
for scaring others away. In the event you got caught and
jailed for such shenanigans, there was a charm for getting
out. To crown it all, there was even a charm for warding off
charms.

These may have been used a lot more than one might
expect. The *Heimskringla*, the history of the old Norse
kings, tells of Finns being tortured to persuade them to cast

a spell that some ruler felt would eliminate his competition.

It's been mentioned that the Finns were happy enough in their innocent animism until missionary fever struck Eric of Sweden. Conversion in those times being expected to include a little wholesome slaughter, those with only luke-warm interest in heaven sometimes arrived there rather suddenly. Along with Bishop Henry, whose martyrdom has been recounted, a number of others had a hand in this Christianity by conquest.

One of them was the revered Saint Olaf. His campaign got a special impetus when an eclipse of the sun, coming at a strategic time, convinced doubters that he had a special rapport with the Almighty. Birgir Jarl, brother-in-law to a Swedish king, subjugated Häme in a bloody expedition, and Torgils Knutson, another Swedish leader, did the same in Karelia. It ended with the Finns cheerfully accepting Christianity, and no doubt that's when they added a Christian tale to the *Kalevala*. Never ones to be sore losers, the Finns made what amends they could to the martyred missionaries. Bishop Henry received the top accolade after being canonized and looks down from heaven upon beautiful Finland as his very own domain. And why not an English patron saint? Saint Patrick was not born in Ireland.

It was during this period in history that the first Finnish churches were built. The cathedral in Turku, a beautiful old building which dates back to the 1200s, is perhaps the best example. Numerous small churches from a long time past are scattered throughout Finland. Some are made from stone, but many are of wood. A particularly elaborate wooden one at Purmo, built in 1722, is still being used.

Finnish Christianity was elemental and straightforward, and like the Finns' former faith it was without fear. Although there were churches and different rituals to be performed, the old festivals honoring the all-important sun as the giver of life were continued, now dignified with the patronage of a Saint Juhannus. The way Christianity was interpreted to the people is shown most charmingly in a fresco of Christ's family tree in the church at Lohja, where the Biblical characters appear dressed in Finnish costume.

The step from Catholicism to Lutheranism was an easy one for the Finns. Gustavus Vasa, their Swedish king and overlord, began the process in the early part of the sixteenth century when he took for himself judicial and administrative functions of the church and began seizing church lands. Lutheranism gained a foothold during the tenure of Michael Agricola, Bishop of Turku, who had studied in Wittenberg, where Martin Luther had nailed his Ninety-Five Theses to the church door.

The bloody religious upheavals of the Reformation had no counterpart in Finland. Either the Finns were too law-abiding to do anything other than accept what was decreed, or else the new religion appealed to them. Certainly they must have approved of abolishing the secular power of the church, since they never took kindly to interference. In any case, the Finns themselves carried out the Reformation within their borders, and there wasn't much reforming involved. Because Catholicism had never been widespread and because paganism still flourished in remote areas, the fresh doctrine replaced the old faith without bloodshed. Those in the outlands hardly noticed the difference.

Michael Agricola had been a peasant lad himself, and he was a believer in moderate reform. While in charge of a school for training young clergymen, he saw the need for bringing the teachings of the church to the people in the vernacular. As a first step, he prepared an ABC book—the first book ever in the Finnish language. He wrote a grammar book, too, and then a prayer book. Finally he translated the New Testament and parts of the Old Testament. Religion was central to the lives of the people, so this important work, long before any other Finnish literature came into being, is a significant landmark. It shows a compassionate concern for those who had no education even in Swedish, the polite language of the time. The Word could be brought to these people only in the familiar speech of their own locality. We must give the church credit for fostering education so that the people might become Bible readers and carry out the Lutheran intention that they themselves should read and understand the Word of God. Besides the cathedral (which is still the seat of the Finnish Lutheran Church), Turku also had a university. So, along with canonical pursuits, the church encouraged cultural developments.

The Reformation saw state churches established in European countries, and Finland was no exception. The Evangelical Lutheran faith is still the official religion of Finland.

But there is no religious coercion. As the Finns see it, there is no religion without freedom, just as there is no freedom without religion. The church is independent of the state, though it is state supported. Perhaps it is more accurate to call it a national church rather than a state church, since the state exerts so little influence on it and church laws, unless they are supported by national laws, are not legally binding.

In an atmosphere of such permissiveness, it may sometimes be difficult for a pastor to convince his flock of the need for churchgoing. A case in point was an old fellow known as Uncle Pekka, a far-from-sterling character who was derelict in many other things besides his church attendance. In the company of farmers thankfully remarking on the good harvest weather, Uncle Pekka startled everyone by claiming the credit. The fine weather had come, he said, because he had prayed for it.

The pastor was amused that such a one as Uncle Pekka should lay claim to influence with the Almighty.

"Did you say we have the good weather because *you* prayed for it?"

Uncle Pekka averred that this was so.

"Why do you think you should get what you pray for? I don't expect to get everything I pray for."

"Well," explained Uncle Pekka modestly, "I don't bother Him all the time."

After Martin Luther put across the idea that Christians were capable of reading the Bible for themselves, a number of minor offshoots cropped up in Finland. Each faction pinpointed some facet of doctrine it thought had been ignored. Some insisted that public confession of sins was the only basis for religious fellowship, since only through complete openness could there be trust among the faithful. Some placed emphasis on being reborn through an ecstatic vision. Some claimed that the Biblical exhortation to "pray without ceasing" meant kneeling in prayer at least fifteen or twenty times a day. There was even a group who maintained that such frivolities as music have no place in a worship service. The latter sternly repressed all colorful language, all ornamentation, and all rhythm or organ accompaniment and insisted that men and women should be sternly segregated, sitting on opposite sides of the church. It was due to this repressive attitude that the *kantele*, the treasured harp of Finland, fell into disuse. Opposition of the church to the revival of the old pagan hero-tales, even in the guise of literature, created difficulties for Elias Lönnrot, collector and compiler of the *Kalevala*.

Some of these ideas were carried to the New World by their adherents, and even today there are austere old Finnish churches where unaccompanied responses are chanted in eerie monotones.

For centuries the Finns were ardent worshipers, and they did not always require a church. Outdoor services were popular and still are. Today there are many outdoor weddings, with Juhannus, or Midsummer Day, the preferred date.

An outdoor fertility ritual was practiced as recently as the eighteenth century, in which the statue of Saint Martin was taken from the church and carried around the plowed fields in a festive procession. It took place on the date of a former pagan feast of fertility. The often-seen decorative motif that is now known as *hannunvaakuna*, or Saint Hans's cross, was at first a magic sign carved on barns and houses to give protection from wizards.

The Finns may have given up their belief in wizards when Christianity arrived, but those in other lands were unable to give up their conviction that the Finns had supernatural powers. Richard Dana, Jr., in *Two Years Before the Mast* reported that the cook on his ship was particularly good to the Finns in deference to their special powers over wind and storm. He told of a Finn who had a bottle of rum that, however often he imbibed, remained half full. It was rumored that Finn ships had been seen sailing against head winds in defiance of nature.

We have corroboration of this talent from no less an expert than Saint Olaf. When he tried to dispense the true religion to the Finns, they not only most ungraciously shot arrows at him all day, but they also used their witchcraft to stir up bad weather at night so that his fleet barely made it home. This opinion was reinforced by Herman Melville, who in *Omoo* stated that Finns had second sight and could wreak supernatural vengeance. To top it off, we hear from Knut Hamsun (a Norwegian novelist who should have known) that a smiling Lapp was an evil omen of such power there was no way one could overcome it.

We never hear these claims from the Finns themselves. As far as they are concerned, the shamanism of long ago, with its reliance on the magic power of words and spells, is long forgotten. According to the *Kalevala*, it came to an end with the first baptism performed by Virokannas and the disgruntled leavetaking of Väinämöinen.

A Finn's religion is a personal thing, and as such not to be closely scrutinized or dissected. The reserved Nordics do not find it easy to say what is in their hearts. Their commitment is private.

A pastor visited an old Finn, a pillar of the church, now on his deathbed, and tenderly offered to pray with him. The old fellow looked at him steadily.

"No, thanks, Pastor," he said. "I don't need your help. I can say my own prayers."

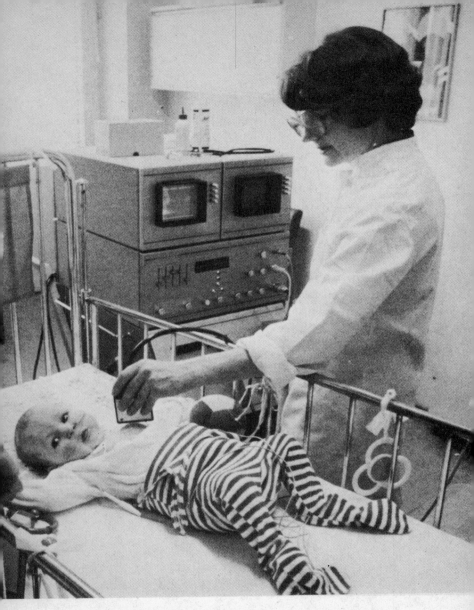

A children's clinic offers the best in medical and nursing care.

CHAPTER 10

MEDICINE, FOLK AND OTHERWISE

BABIES HAVE NOTHING to say about where they will be born, but if they were offered a choice, no doubt they would pick Finland. Finland has always given high priority to the health of children, and infant mortality statistics reflect this. Finland's rate is ten deaths per thousand live births, one of the lowest in the world, and a model for any nation. To be born in Finland is to have the best of chances to survive.

So now we come to another genuine Finnish paradox. How does one explain that along with the healthiest babies in the world, Finland has the highest mortality rates for later ages among the developed nations? If Finland's rate for middle-aged men is stated as 100, the other Nordic countries have rates as low as 25. A list of thirty-two countries, with England in the middle at 100, puts Finland at the top with 124. The leading causes of death in Finland are heart disease and cancer. If you are a man, you may expect to live 65.4 years, and women hold out for 72.6. Suicide, too, takes its toll. A grim statistic is that nearly 20 out of 100,000 give up before their time as suicides, and Finland is the "leading" country in deaths from this cause.

These are shattering facts. They do not at all reflect Finland's great concern for health as shown in its effective health services and care, extensive national sickness insurance, five medical schools, and widespread primary health and dental care policies. With 12 percent of the population being cared for at public expense and an annual health care expenditure of four hundred dollars per person, we find it hard to discover a reason for these disturbing statistics.

Another serious medical problem is alcoholism. The Finns' drinking habits and capacity are at once the envy and despair of other serious drinkers. Finns have tried to combat the problem by supporting temperance unions for nearly one hundred years, and there was a period of national prohibition that was no more successful than it was here. Controlling the sale of alcoholic beverages through a state-owned monopoly, Alcoholiliike Oy, provides some restraint. (Though this has given rise to a plaintive joke: "Alcohol, I like—oh, why?") Finns are indeed serious drinkers. Seven percent of the consumer's income goes for alcohol, to support an average annual consumption of 6.2 litres per person. Attempts to substitute wine for hard liquor have resulted only in more wine being drunk without any decrease in the amount of stronger alcoholic beverages. Not surprisingly, Finland has perhaps the most progressive treatment of alcoholics to be found anywhere, and its methods are often studied by other countries.

We can understand the Finns' concern. Alcoholism is an illness that imposes a burden on the taxpayers, particularly in a nation with socialized health care. It also causes other serious social problems such as drunken driving and crimes of violence. It is sobering to note that 10 percent of the drinkers account for 50 percent of the drinks.

Finland's health services—and problems—are clearly on a par with those of other nations having a technologically advanced, complex society. The Finns have a history of being preoccupied with science and learning. One of their leaders in the field of biochemistry, A.I. Virtanen, was awarded the Nobel Prize in 1945 for his studies on human nutrition and cattle feeding. There are medical schools in

Tampere, Kuopio, and Oulu as well as Turku and Helsinki. There has never been a shortage of nurses, although one appears to be developing now. As in our own backwoods areas, however, twentieth-century medicine in Finland has had a long way to come.

A hardy people, the Finns had little need for doctors except at times of accident or epidemics. The epidemics of years past were terrible in their effects, laying low whole families or villages. The bubonic plague of the 1300s wiped out a third of Finland's inhabitants. Smallpox was a dreaded scourge, as was diphtheria, which struck the young most severely and caused terror in the hearts of parents who were helpless against its onslaught. We have no way of measuring the number of hearts weakened by scarlet fever, which was greatly feared in the nineteenth century for its hideous trail of aftereffects.

There were skilled doctors, at least in the cities. Lönnrot was one, and the universities of Turku and Helsinki turned out many others. There were also those who learned their skills by being apprenticed to physicians already in practice. Learning to be a doctor in those days involved feeding the teacher's horse as well as watching while he lanced a boil. Whatever he knew was what the aspiring physician learned. The doctor who took an apprentice did so as much from a need for a handyman as from a desire to impart his skills.

Physicians were not numerous, and in remote areas a doctor was as big a curiosity as a two-headed calf. Under such circumstances, to call a doctor was to admit that the patient was at the pearly gates with one foot on a banana peel. One oldster recalls only two such dire cases during his lifetime: a farmer gored by a bull and a hunter whose flintlock exploded in his face.

By and large, home cure was the rule if any cure was possible. Medicine was rough and ready. Czar Alexander was told in 1819 that the only cures used in Finland were a gulp of whiskey, a pipeful of tobacco, and the vapors of the sauna.

The sauna was a lifesaver, indeed, and in important ways served as a hospital, for every household had one. It was really a better hospital than those available in most of the world. A sauna was clean—exceptionally so—from the heat, steam, and soap and water. The warmth brought relaxation as well as cleanliness so that the sauna was actually an ideal place for giving birth. Many Finns aren't joking when they say, "I was born in a sauna."

A loyal Finn will tell you that he or she goes to the sauna to cure boils, sunburn, near-pneumonia, fevers, rheumatism, chilblains, infection, arthritis, insomnia, gout, poor circulation, and a broken heart. Does it sound like snake oil? The queer part of it is that sauna therapy seems to work. A doubter scorched by sunburn has only to give it a try to find that the sauna seems to relieve his misery and even fade his color. Many is the cold sufferer who went sniffling and hoarse to the sauna in the evening and arose clear headed and syrup voiced the following morning. The rate of cure may not be 100 percent, but after all, does any doctor claim a perfect record?

Other home remedies, some more painful and more fragrant than the sauna, have been tried by those without recourse to modern medicine. An old country Finn will tell you with a straight face that allowing yourself to be stung repeatedly by bees or burying yourself in an anthill brings relief from rheumatism. Another traditional cure is to immure yourself in a manure pile. The heat generated from the chemical reactions therein allegedly releases certain beneficial vapors, driving them through the skin into the joints or bones affected, thus effecting a cure. Vapors certainly emerge, beneficial or not. It has not been unknown, even in this country, to see a head emerging from the manure pile adjacent to most barns, while smoke from the calmly resting patient's pipe ascends with the other aromas.

Another cure which, like the sauna and the manure pile, was historically in plentiful supply was pine tar. It was used for colds and respiratory ailments, and the fact that a number of modern manufacturers feel it is a valuable part of their cough remedy formula points to its effectiveness. Since coughs, pneumonia, and bronchitis were prevalent in a climate such as Finland's, pine tar was, of course, on everyone's medicine shelf. No doubt it helped that the substance was produced in abundance—if the prescription didn't do any good, at least it was cheap.

Whiskey or spirits were used as a medicine in every nation in which they could be found, and Finland was no exception. Humans learned early to make alcoholic liquors from whatever they had handy. If nothing else, a bit of booze made the patient a little braver or perhaps anesthetized him so that he thought he felt better. Of course, there were side effects. As the Finns put it, "A drink of whiskey makes you a new man—and that new man is thirsty too."

It goes without saying that hangovers are still a common illness. Favorite home cures are raw egg, pickles, or buttermilk. A sauna, of course, is recommended by many, though doctors advise a cold shower and nausea pills such as dramamine. A breakfast with a sugared drink and bread to absorb the alcohol may do the job, or you may get help from salt fish or meat. The most efficacious cure, alas, is alcohol itself. That is as far as we have come since the Assyrians gave us advice on how to treat a hangover, thirty-five hundred years ago.

With home remedies available, the home physician of yesterday had little need for other medicines, although in every community there were those who understood the curative power of herbs. In an emergency these wise people would be called upon, but the average person had faith in the Big Three. There was a saying: "If spirits, tar, and sauna avail nothing, there is no cure."

Sometimes, when no other human help succeeded, it was necessary to fall back on the ministrations of the *kupparimummu*. This was an old woman whose art was the letting of blood, which was thought to release the noxious poisons that were causing the illness.

From one standpoint it was not altogether wrong. Blood should and does renew itself. Doctors tell us that a transfusion may benefit a healthy donor as well as the recipient, since it permits the renewal of blood cells and it does no harm to reduce the quantity of blood slightly. Taking blood from sick persons, however, is an entirely different matter, and it has been more than a century since such therapy for illness has been considered legitimate.

The kupparimummu, or "cupping woman," was quite professional in her ministrations, bringing with her the tools of her calling: a small, sharp scalpel with which to make the incisions and small cups that were applied to the cuts to suck out the blood. Of course, she had no license, at least not after World War I, but that did not prevent her from being called in by the family, who had faith in her judgment. People might often fear and distrust the doctor, whose learning set him apart, but the kupparimummu was one of their own. In a clash of treatments, they were likely to believe her, and the backwoods are full of tales in which the doctor was baffled but the kupparimummu saved the patient. On her part she was likely to be jealous of her professional standing, speaking with scorn of "newfangled ideas" promulgated by those having heads full of book knowledge who lacked the sense to appreciate her science.

Her handmaiden, the *hieroanta* ("masseuse"), wasn't

nearly so controversial. Her skill might be needed if a bone was dislocated or a muscle strained. She yanked and pounded mercilessly, and people frequently avoided calling on her until all else had failed. But her treatments helped, perhaps on the principle that it felt so good when she stopped.

This is by no means the state of medical science in Finland now. Americans who have suffered illness or accident and needed hospital care while visiting Finland are consistent in singing the praises of Finnish medical care. Not only are the doctors skilled and abreast of the latest medical techniques, but the nursing is also superior. The percentage of doctors to the general population is high, and all of the miracle operations may be performed there. The European Dialysis and Transplant Association held its fourteenth annual congress in Finlandia Hall in 1977. Organ transplants are no new marvel in Finland. The five-hundredth kidney transplant was performed several years ago and more than one hundred such operations are done in any given year. Finnish surgeons would double the number if there were enough suitable donors. The fact that the Nordic countries maintain a systematic exchange of compatible organs helps to relieve the shortage.

We might continue with a recital of facts and figures on the Finnish medical scene, but let's not. The point is clear. If Finns have problems, their wizards can handle them.

Finland is famous worldwide for its wood products and the excellence of its beautifully designed consumer goods.

CHAPTER 11

SOMETIMES GOLD IS GREEN

WE HAVE SEEN that Finland is a rather sparsely settled land of lowlands and forests. Except for copper, it lacks substantial mineral resources and has no supplies of oil, natural gas, or coal. How then do we account for the fact that Finland has a per capita income of $5620, a figure not far below the affluent United States at $7060, and is the fifteenth most prosperous nation in the world?

Let's take an economist's eye view and survey the Finns at work to find out how their prosperity came about.

Although the days when every peasant worked the land are long past, about a fifth of Finland's people are still farmers and they produce about 6 percent of the national income. We must balance this against the fact that a tenth of Finland's cropland was ceded to Russia during World War II. Still, if the remaining arable land was divided, each person would have 1.4 acres. About 40 percent of Finland's population is rural.

Gardeners may wonder what can be grown in the cold, stony soil. The Finns were as eager as anyone to adopt the New World's contribution, the potato. It's a good crop for northern areas and has been promoted as a valuable possibility for Lapland. Nature has been kind to Lapland in that there are no insect pests or weeds with which to contend, and Finland has established an agricultural experiment station north of the Arctic Circle. Crops grown in the south include oats, barley, rye, turnips, beets, and a variety of vegetables. Fruit is limited though there are many varieties of berries, both wild and cultivated.

The growing season is short, but the long summer days, seventy-three of them having continuous daylight, do much to make up the difference. Farmers can expect from fifteen to thirty inches of rainfall in a year.

Dairying is a natural industry in a country with lush greenery. It shouldn't surprise us that the Finns made this a mainstay of their economy long ago. Taxes in 1260 were paid in butter, and butter was extolled as a lip-smacking delicacy in the ancient *Kalevala*.

A hundred years ago, most farming was diversified. The farmer raised a little wheat, a little barley, a little rye, a few vegetables and, of course, he had a cow or two. It was after the serious grain famine of 1868–1869 that the Finns saw the need for more intensive farming, and after several decades in which dairying grew increasingly important, Valio, a cooperative dairy association, was formed. Dairying benefited so much from Valio's research work on everything from cattle feed to marketing that it now accounts for two-thirds of the agricultural income.

Finland still exports butter, but its quantity is now almost matched by the exports of cheese and dried milk. The Finns keep enough milk for themselves, however, to consume 250 quarts of milk per person per year. That's a pint and a half a day each! As for cheese, consumption has increased so rapidly that it even tripled in one year. Favorites are Edam and Emmenthal. Emmenthal, originally the cheese of the Swiss mountains, was traditionally made with nine-tenths superstition and one-tenth knowledge, but the Finns have reversed that to nine-tenths science and one-tenth art. Their formula is so successful that they can even sell "Swiss" cheese in Austria and Italy.

The traditional Finnish delicacy *viili* (yogurt) is produced in prodigious quantities for home consumption, but alas for the world, it doesn't take kindly to being exported. If you'd like to try your hand at making your own, see the recipe on page 175.

Finnish economists emphasize the value of dual-purpose cows, which supply both milk and meat so that Finland doesn't need to import beef or veal. Finland's expertise in cattle breeding is much studied by other countries.

One drawback to progress is that since individual farms are small, it is poor economy to take the step which has been the saving of American agriculture: heavy mechanization. Some automation is in use, of course, but it is unnecessary in small holdings. As a consequence, the visitor may enjoy the nostalgic sight of hay drying on crossed poles even today. Another disadvantage of farming in Finland is that cattle must be indoors six or eight months of the year. Large barns and abundant hay storage are necessities. Except for "know-how," Finland isn't in a position to export nondairy agricultural products but at least the country manages to be almost self-sufficient in most areas, and the Finns even produce a surplus of bread grains. This has a special significance, for Finland has known famine within the last one hundred fifty years, when the backwoods people mixed pine bark with their grain to make bread.

Though agriculture is alive and well, it isn't what makes Finland's economy strong.

Just a look at the countryside of Finland will show us the chief basis of the economy. Finland has a unique resource: "green gold," or, if you want to say it in Finnish, *vihreä kulta.* More than 70 percent of the country is forested; of these areas, 44 percent is pine, 38 percent spruce, and the remaining 18 percent is deciduous, mostly birch.

One of the nicest things about "green gold" is that it is

renewable, and the Finns know how to get the most out of it. They have learned how to balance the conflicting demands of economics and environmental concerns so that the serene forests do not look scarred or depleted, and yet they are able to furnish more than 50 percent of Finland's exports. The government has set up a tax structure that makes it profitable for even a small landowner to be a tree farmer. Crop farming goes hand-in-hand with timber production. The Finn who wears the broad hat of the farmer in summer dons a lumberman's hard hat in winter.

The tar boats of long ago have disappeared, along with the picturesque log drives, and perhaps it is just as well. Imagine taking three weeks to make your way upstream to the pineries, spending the winter boiling pitch from mounds of pine logs and decanting it into barrels which you made, and then whizzing downstream with it over fast, swirling rapids in a boat forty feet long and barely wide enough for two men. Like most activities in connection with logging, tar making may have looked picturesque, but it involved a high level of strength and coordination, as well as grueling hard work and daring. As a by-product of charcoal making, it has lost its importance and now other returns from timber production undergird the industries of Finland.

Today Finland ranks fourth in the world in the production of paper for export and fifth in wood. Finnish newsprint alone is exported to 130 countries, and Finland is the world's leading producer of plywood. Savonlinna boasts the world's largest plywood mill while the city of Lahti holds the global record for the most furniture factories.

Finland has an economy that falls somewhere between "mixed" and free enterprise with the emphasis on free enterprise. The railroad, telephone and telegraph, and postal systems are owned by the state as is Alcoholiliike, the state monopoly on liquors. Other state-owned enterprises, such as those in copper mining and iron and steel production, are not subsidized to keep them solvent. The fact that they must compete with privately owned companies does a lot to keep the bureaucracy slim and trim.

Sometime before 1900 there appeared a Finnish phenomenon that became so firmly entrenched in the country's economics, it has even been exported. Moreover, it has flourished in this country wherever Finns have a community. This is the cooperative, or "co-op." The establishment of cooperative stores was successful early in this century, beginning with central societies which supplied stores with merchandise and manufactured such diverse goods as matches, bicycles, bricks, and clothing. Canning factories and coffee-roasting plants were added, machinery for the group was imported, laboratories were set up to develop new products, and sales analysts were set to the task of finding new markets.

The farmers' co-ops work toward filling their special needs: buying and selling machinery (and maintaining foreign offices for this purpose) and processing and marketing crops. They also operate experimental stations, nurseries, flour mills, and machine shops. The situation is somewhat comparable to the way in which the U.S. Agricultural Extension Service works in research and development.

Finland's transportation systems are modern and efficient. More than a million cars buzz around Finland's highways, which make every part of the country accessible. It works out to a car for every third man, woman, or child. An unfortunate portion of the roads are unsurfaced or surfaced just enough to hide the rocks, but if you want to "get there from here," you certainly can.

Since the first train puffed its way through the countryside in 1861, Finland's iron roads have grown to a 3600-mile network that spans the country. Along with other West

European nations, Finland offers a special Finnrail pass to foreigners, who may travel for two weeks in a dizzy whirl, wherever they wish to go in Finland for sixty dollars or so.

There's a densely netted airline system as well, so if you care to cover the same ground as your railway-riding friend, you may do so for barely double the cost. There are twenty domestic airports in Finland, and planes fly to twenty-eight foreign destinations as well. The hydrofoils and lake steamers that ply the inland waterways add a touch of novelty for travelers who come from less watery lands.

It doesn't take an economist to figure out that fisheries are important in a nation blessed with a long ocean coastline and a lake district in which lakes cover half of the total area. Would you believe 160 million Finnmarks? There are almost seven thousand deep-sea fishing boats, nearly all of which are small vessels. Fishing is not just a national pastime, it's a lucrative business as well.

In this connection, it might be noted that Finland claims Ole Evinrude, the father of motor boating.

The shipyards of Rauma Repola Oy rival anything of the kind, anywhere. Want a new pleasure yacht? At Pietasaari in north Finland, racing craft are built by hand with unbeatable results. A yacht with a plastic body built in Turku is so popular that 85 percent of the factory's output is snatched up by foreigners.

A country which depends on its export trade for one-fourth of its paycheck is bound to have a fine merchant marine. Finland's fleet totals 439 vessels, including steamers, tankers, and lesser craft. During World War II the Soviet Union demanded 365,000 tons of shipping vessels, a stunning blow when one considers that Finland's total for the ten years before the war was 23,000 tons. The quota was met and so, in a way, the Finns can thank Russia for their shipbuilding industry. They can also credit their superior production. It was either that or some special spellbinding charm that recently made it possible for the Finnish envoy to convince the Russians that their next ice breaker should be made in Finland. He did it with just ten words!

Whether the Russians' boost was welcome at first or not, their demands for engineering goods and machinery had the stupendous result of bringing Finland's gross national product of 1965 to double that of pre-World War II.

The most striking facet of Finland's meteoric postwar rise is in the field of industrial design. Young designers have taken the ordinary things of day-to-day living and given them a bold, new, clean look that goes back to basic forms. In their revolutionary styling of articles that have looked the same for generations, these designing Finns have produced household items that are functional and yet streamlined with such beauty of form and joyful color that they are exhibited around the world as works of art. They've done it with scissors, glassware, flatware, and fabrics.

The first example we think of in this eye-satisfying category is the rya rug. (It's really *ryijy*, but there's no need to struggle with the word; it's pronounced "rya" everywhere.) These rugs are hand woven on pedal looms. Bold designs are worked in the traditional manner, with several strands of yarn being knotted with the special rya knot onto a backing. The effect of tone on tone or contrast is accomplished by the adroit blending of the yarns, and the swirling effect of the varied earth colors—sometimes as many as five in one long shaggy fall of yarn—creates beautiful artistic effects. They were once made to keep fishermen warm with the long, heavy pile, but by the eighteenth century they were already recognized as an art form. Not surprisingly, they are more in demand as wall hangings than as foot wipers. A leading designer of rya rugs is Kirsti Ilvessalo.

Fabrics in themselves are a noteworthy branch of industrial art. Here forceful color in large, clean areas is the dominant note. Finnish fabrics have a gaiety and spontaneity that offers a contrast to the simple, stripped-down shapes of furniture and utensils. The vivid, splashy textiles complement the simplicity of the Finns' lifestyle and form a natural antidote to their other penchant, a leaning toward coarse textures, natural materials, and earth tones. It all looks new and young and brave.

Marimekko is a success story that has often been told. It began in 1949 as a small oilcloth factory run by an ex-army major. It wasn't successful, so the company switched to printing fabric. That wasn't successful either until Armi Ratia, the major's wife, came to the rescue. She began to design fabrics that were brightly patterned and unconventional, bringing in young designers who followed her lead. The next step was to make these fabrics into a simple dress that was timeless in its styling. Marimekko's standing in the fashion world was assured when Jacqueline Kennedy bought nine of Armi Ratia's creations. Ratia's son is now the factory's chief designer, and the spirit of Marimekko lives on.

If glass is your interest, there is no country which has produced more innovative designs than Finland. Finnish magic has transformed a plain glass tumbler into a work of art that evokes thoughts of icebergs, fountains, and Northern Lights. Nuutajarvi Glassworks has received many world awards. Iitala Glass, which was one hundred years old in 1981, is now the biggest producer of everyday glass in the Scandinavian countries, thanks to its Paula glass for the table that withstands both heat and cold.

The big name in ceramics is Arabia. It was established as a pottery a hundred years ago and is now the largest such factory in Europe. Though it is part of the great Wärtsilä combine, its works are of beauty rather than power. Here again Finnish designers took off in their own direction, expressing themes of Finland. Tapio Virkkala, Timo Sarpaneva, Rut Bryk, Kyllikki Salmenhaara, Francesca Lindh, and Kaj Franck have all contributed to stunning designs with a fresh, honest look.

The man who has done the most, however, to give the average Finnish home its functional look is Alvar Aalto. An architect of world renown, his work is a monument in itself. His ideas have produced not only large civic buildings such as Finlandia Hall but also homely items like chairs. His philosophy—"First we must build the country, then show it to others"—carries over into things such as lamps, beds, chairs, and cookware so that Finnish Modern has an integrated look. Aalto died in 1976, but the designs of Ilmari Tapiovarra shows that his influence is living still.

The abundance and excellence of Finland's consumer goods point to a high standard of living. With the extensive social programs that are carried out, there is little poverty. Inflation has hit Finland along with the rest of the world, but Finns still enjoy the good life. With their love of simplicity and natural things, there is little or no ostentatious wealth. The banker lives much the same as the laborer and the teacher.

Yes, there is magic in the climb Finland has accomplished. It is a magic compounded of bold design in which old habits of thinking are swept away and simple things are seen with new eyes, a cheerful yet practical assessment of what there is to work with and how best to use it, and the desire to stay clear of the hovering menace of Soviet takeover. Plus, as you can well imagine, a large dash of Finnish sisu. And that, friends, is the real magic of Finland.

The Sibelius monument by Eila Hiltunen in Helsinki.

Chapter 12

MORE FINNISH MAGIC

IT GOES WITHOUT SAYING that there are bound to be people who are revered in Finland and yet unknown to the outside world. It is surprising, however, that a country so small should have someone who ranks among the foremost in almost every field of human endeavor.

Take, for instance, the arts.

An art in which the touch of Finnish magic is indisputable is architecture. More than 150 years ago, the Finns demonstrated that city planning is an attainable ideal.

This may have happened in the natural order of things. The building material closest to hand was wood, so for ages most buildings were made of it. Fine, but the natural enemy of wood is fire, and in a cold country fire is a necessity. If carried too far, a house warming might result in no house at all, and even—since fire-fighting was not the science that it is today—no city. In the early 1800s Turku and Helsinki were destroyed by fire within a decade of each other.

When a city is rebuilt to specifications, it is possible to plan it so that it is better after each disaster. A Swede-Finn named Johann Ehrenstrom drew up a new plan for Helsinki, and the credit for the harmonious transformation goes to Carl Ludwig Engel, a German architect, who set the tone of severe simplicity in the august Senate Square. Engel also planned the rebuilding of Turku. It's particularly remarkable because this was back in the days when planned cities were as unheard-of as planned parenthood.

Since then, any rebuilding is done in the context of what is most appropriate—a maxim that applies to new building as well. An outstanding model city of today is Tapiola, which came into being in the 1950s. It is a small city so artfully built in the midst of woodland that it does not seem to be a city at all.

Building comes naturally to the Finns. Perhaps because their homes are so important to them, they want every corner to reflect beauty and the ultimate in craftsmanship. It is thanks to the Finns that the log cabin, which was so basic in American pioneering, took the form it did. Finnish cabin-building in Delaware spread throughout the colonies, where the distinctive dovetailed corners of the modest structures made them identifiable as Finnish craftsmanship. Later, they were found in the early twentieth-century buildings of Finn immigrant homesteaders.

Most familiar to Americans is a name that is almost a dynasty: Saarinen. Eliel Saarinen first came to public notice with his winning design for the railroad station in Helsinki. In 1922 he won second prize in the contest for the *Chicago Tribune*'s tower with a design that revolutionized the building of skyscrapers. From that time on, his fame was international. He came to America in 1923 and was followed by his son Eero, whose fame was equally great.

Finland's contribution to architecture is felt around the world, and we do not have to go to Finland to see why this is so. The Toronto City Hall was designed by Vilho Reivell, hailed by no less an authority than Frank Lloyd Wright as an outstanding architectural genius. Eero Saarinen created the CBS building in Manhattan, the TWA Flight Center, the terminal at Dulles International Airport, the Saint Louis Arch, and the American embassy in London. Yes, and the IBM building near Rochester, Minnesota, is a Saarinen creation. Alvar Aalto designed a dormitory for MIT in Cambridge, Massachusetts, with an undulating brick wall which was an innovation in the use of brick in rounded forms. And there are others. Buildings all over the world have the mark of Finnish simplicity and boldness of concept. According to Alvar Aalto, whose influence is now felt strongly, "Architecture is so highly regarded in Finland because it is our form of expression, because our language is so impossible."

Aalto has more designs to his credit than can be cited. His master plan for the city of Rovaniemi after its destruction in World War II is spectacular. It has been called "a great gleaming phoenix with concrete feathers." In some ways Aalto's style is a departure from the clean, angular lines of Saarinen and his followers, but that's to be expected. Creative Finns don't copy one another any more than they follow architectural formulas from other lands. (One of the Saarinens, in fact, was heard to speak of "Frank Lloyd Wrong.")

Aalto tried everything with the objective of designing a complete, integrated home environment that would be esthetically satisfying. He originated styles in tables and chairs, vases, benches, lamps, and stools. There are twenty Aalto buildings in Finland and numerous houses which, he said, had to meet four important criteria: They must represent the persons who live in them; they must suit their life-style; they must have a psychological impact; and they must have a feeling of love. He liked a sense of peace and openness.

Finland's giant in music is world famous, too. Johan Julius Sibelius, known as Jean Sibelius, was at his death in 1957 the greatest composer in the world. Incredibly enough, in one masterly piece of music, he has captured the soul of Finland—the grandeur of forests and fells, the stern beauty of the winters, the gay lakes and rivers—and with it the freedom-loving spirit of the Finns. This composition, the· tone poem *Finlandia,* is beloved by the Finns but almost anyone can recognize the spirit he conveys of worship for the beauties of the land and rocklike determination to keep it from being despoiled.

Sibelius was not an artist who starved in a garret, for he came from a family of cultured, well-to-do Finns, with a good proportion of Swedish blood. (But he thought of himself as all Finn!) His talent was recognized early, and while he was still a young man, he was awarded a government pension that enabled him to devote his time solely to music.

Sibelius composed a number of works based on the *Kalevala.* The beautiful symphony he named after Kullervo, one of the epic's heroes, was acclaimed instantly, but for some reason Sibelius refused to let it be performed a second time. It was not heard again until after his death. Though his music has melody, it is modernistic rather than conservative, relying only a little on rhythmic effects. Perhaps best known, next to *Finlandia,* is "Valse Triste," haunting and poignant.

To be appreciated by your own people in your own time is rare enough, but the works of Sibelius are remarkable for any composer. And he is only one of a long procession of Finns who contributed to their country's and the world's musical heritage. Although *Finlandia* is sung for patriotic occasions (and at other times) throughout Finland, the national anthem was written by another, much earlier. Johan Ludwig Runeberg, whose poem was written so long ago that the original text was in Swedish, called his work "Vårtland" ("Our Land"). In Finnish it is known as "Maamme," which means the same thing, but whichever language it's sung in, the sentiment is totally Finnish! The uplifting melody was composed by Fredrik Pacius. You'll find the whole composition, in both languages, in the appendix.

Other composers of note who have come out of Finland include Toivo Kuula, whose music is as rugged as Sibelius's, but with more pathos; Leevi Madetoja, with more soulful compositions; Erkki Melartin; Selim Palmgren; and Uuno Klami.

The Finns' musical instrument is the kantele, a five-stringed harp which the old bard Väinämöinen made of birch. This original instrument was widely copied in birch or pine and hung on the wall in readiness for rune singing. In modern times a renewed interest in Finnish folklore brought about larger instruments, elaborate and complex. By 1813 the kantele had eighteen strings, and now it boasts thirty-six. The limpid music of this instrument defies description. It may be plaintive or passionate, gently simple or bewilderingly complex. There are experts who perform with skill in Finland, notably Ula Katiavuori, who have done much to revive the art. There's even a small coterie of kantele players in the United States. Melvin Kangas at Suomi College in Hancock, Michigan, is a master of the Finnish harp.

Finns eventually got the violin, too, and there is nowhere a more solidly Finnish folk music tradition than at Kaustinen, where several hundred violinists join the Purpuripelimannit players in a festival of haunting, delicate music, much of it in a minor key.

Most often we think of the accordian as the best accompaniment to Finnish folksongs, and its hearty gaiety is found on most folk dance records. All of these never-forgotten songs and dances are enjoying a rebirth, and you'll see them at many summer festivals, adding their color and exuberance to the scene.

Finland has a national opera house, which is located in

Helsinki, and every fall its performances are featured in the Helsinki Festival, along with other cultural events ranging from ballet to art exhibitions, drama, and films.

An opera composed in 1975 in honor of the five-hundredth anniversary of Olavinlinna (Olaf's castle) won the Nordic Council's 1978 Composition Prize. This opera, called *The Horsemen,* was written by Aulis Sallinen and tells of war, destiny, and death in medieval Finland. In 1968, another Finn, Joonas Kokkonen, was awarded the Nordic prize for his Third Symphony.

Finland's musical traditions, of course, result in choirs and choruses who perform internationally. The Children's Choir of Tapiola, under the direction of Erkki Pohjola, is a favorite everywhere in Finland and has won recognition abroad with UNICEF choir tours. Much of their repertoire is the work of Finnish composers, some of whom (including Kokkonen, mentioned above) write music especially for the choir.

The literature of Finland got a late but strong start in the nineteenth-century awakening of national fervor. One author whose work can be read in English is Alexis Kivi, a sort of Finnish Dickens whose novel, *Seven Brothers*, was a departure from the more formal literary traditions. Kivi was a contemporary of Mark Twain, and like him, he celebrated native wit and perseverance. His heroes were seven men who were what we would have to call boneheads. Teachers now might say that they had a mental block, for struggle as they might, they could not learn to read. This was crucial, for a Finnish law of long-standing forbade the marriage of anyone who was illiterate. The agonies of the brothers as they struggled with the alphabet and the most elementary instruction were hilarious. Finally, after much sweating and head-banging, it dawned on them one by one that the little bugs on the page were a, and b, and c! Like Lönnrot, Alexis

Kivi was the son of an inebriate tailor, and his earthy, realistic novel reflected a view of life that was unusual in the literature of his day.

The poetry of Eino Leino, who was born eight years after Kivi's death in 1870, was truly Finnish in feeling. Independence was his theme—both for his nation and the individual. Like many Finnish writers, he was strongly influenced by the *Kalevala.*

There are others who have achieved international distinction by their writing. Frans Eemil Sillanpää was the first Finnish writer to win the Nobel Prize for literature in 1939. Two of his novels, *Fallen Asleep While Young* and *Meek Heritage*, have been translated into English. The latter is especially noteworthy because of its emotional impact and its treatment of the civil war, a conflict that is almost unknown beyond Finland's borders. Instead of a panoramic political novel, however, *Meek Heritage* is the story of a born loser whose life begins in poverty and ends by chance. Another great Finnish writer, Väinö Linna, won the Nordic Literature Prize of 1963 for his novel, *The Unknown Soldier.* Set in the Finnish Winter War, it is a sardonic and wry commentary on the little irritations of war, much in the spirit of Bill Mauldin's *Up Front.*

One step beyond, picturing the absolute futility of war and its absurdity as a means of political decision making, is *The Manila Rope,* a novel by Veijo Meri. We come full circle with *Beria's Gardens,* Unto Parvelahti's account of Soviet concentration camps, which derives black humor from utter misery.

A recent author whose name should be familiar to American readers is Mika Waltari. His novels are magnificent historical panoramas, so thoroughly researched as to give one a feeling of being there. *Sinuhe The Egyptian* has as its central character a weak-spirited physician who might have been the real heir to Egypt's throne, but who learns about this and about integrity too late. In *The Wanderer*, a Finn named Michael meets slavery and brutality in the clutches of Moslem pirates during the fifteenth-century wars.

Promising young writers in Finland include Lassi Sinkkonen, the author of *Solveig's Song*, the story of a girl in war-torn Helsinki, and Heikki Turunen, whose books depict the country people of North Karelia in a humorous, elemental style reminding one of Erskine Caldwell.

Painters, too, Finland has in plenty. Some are romantic and easily interpreted, some crude and robust, and others vigorously modern in a way that is distinctly Finnish. The world first noted Albert Edelfelt's work. His portrait of Pasteur at work hangs in the Louvre. He also gained a reputation for his simple, old-fashioned scenes of peasants and fishermen. The credit for being the first important painter goes to R. V. Ekman. His work has not passed the test of time, but his name stands as another figure in the nationalist movement, proclaiming to the world that Finland had painters.

Intense nationalism is also shown in the canvasses of Akseli Gallen-Kallela, which illustrate the *Kalevala* with sweep and power. Their powerful, vigorous figures, filled with drama and emotion, are unforgettable. Then there is Hugo Sinberg, whose irreverent humor and symbolism remind one of Alexis Kivi's comic originality in his novels and plays. Although Tapio Tapiovarra is known as the artist of the Finnish labor movement, his works transcend politics. His *Kalevala* mural shows in mosaic the building of the sampo. With arresting symbolism it shows the figures as stocky, modern workmen. Finland's national museum, the Athenaeum, exhibits these and other works indigenous to Finland in their preoccupation with naturalistic Finnish subjects, wry humor, and robust themes.

At least two Lapp painters, Reidar Sarestoniemi and Andreas Alariesto, have had collections of their works published. Their paintings show the spirit and color of Lapland, its old tales, its spirits, fells, and animals.

Sculpture is second nature to the Finns. Statues of Alexander II, the only Russian whom Finland so honors, and the national poet Johan Ludwig Runeberg, were both done by Runeberg's son, Walter. A striking statue in the modern manner is Väinö Aaltonen's rendition of the Olympic runner Paavo Nurmi, an example of perfect balance on one foot. More Finnish in feeling are his works in granite. On the Tampere Bridge are figures depicted in action so charged with emotion that they almost seem to move. Aaltonen's stunning war memorial of a kneeling soldier and his stark figures of brave boys and girls further assure his international reputation. Eila Hiltunen created the Sibelius monument, a modernistic assembly of silvery pipes. The most innovative sculpture is now being done in glass and ceramics, the media Teemo Luoto has chosen for his whimsical, enchanting animal figures.

Wood sculpture, too, is frequently seen in Finland. Much of it is crudely humorous in intent — sauna scenes abound — but some wood carvings rise above buffoonery and become delightful. The wood sculpture of Yrjo Rosola rightfully takes its place as art.

With all its diversity, there is a certain unity in Finnish art. The nontraditional outlook, the bare-bones beauty, the love of nature, all say "Finland." In this as in all else, the Finn listens to a drummer of his own.

The sauna is a family affair.

CHAPTER 13

SOME LIKE IT HOT

FOR THOSE WHO STILL argue about which came first, the chicken or the egg, there is another philosophical question. Did the Finns develop the sauna, or did the sauna develop the Finns? Did their hardihood and endurance result from using these palaces of torture, as they appear to the uninitiated, or did the Finns devise the sauna as a testing ground because they already were that way? Nobody knows. Since the sauna has been a part of Finnish culture for the past two thousand years or more, it is an inseparable element in the formation of the Finnish character.

"Sauna" has become a household word. We no longer have to teach neophytes that the word is pronounced "sowna," with the first syllable rhyming with "now." Most people know something of what a sauna is like and have experienced what they fondly imagine is its true nature in a motel or club. Unless they are of Finnish extraction or in the company of those who are, it's all too likely that what they have enjoyed is a very much watered-down version of the old Finnish custom.

Is it a custom? Sometimes the sauna assumes the importance of a tribal rite or a social occasion. There's widespread disagreement as to the exact position it occupies in Finnish life, but one thing is certain. It's distinctly Finnish, and it's emphatically integral. There are in Finland no less than six hundred thousand private saunas and many public ones. At least eight out of ten homes have a sauna, preferably by a lake. No wonder Finnish skins are clean, clean, clean!

Cleanliness as a national ideal is something of a historical novelty. In the drafty castles of Western Europe even great ladies seldom bathed in winter. Our own nation is barely a hundred years past the time when small children might be sewed into their underwear from fall to spring, and the daily bath didn't become popular until the advent of indoor plumbing. How unlikely, then, that the fetish of inner and outer cleansing should be clung to so stubbornly by these self-directed people close by the Arctic Circle, while more sophisticated nations shrugged their grimy shoulders and accepted personal cleanliness as the privilege of the wealthy.

Even people living in mixed communities looked askance at the mysterious building behind a Finnish neighbor's house, which they referred to as the "Finn bath," and continued to be aromatic. It took the exposure of our athletes to the benefits it gave to the Olympic contenders from Finland to start us thinking, "Maybe there is something in it." A few brave, adventurous souls tried it—and presto!—the sauna acquired status as a new toy for the wealthy.

So what is a sauna? The earliest ones were dug into the side of a hill or a sloped area of ground. The word itself comes from a word meaning dugout. No Finn was too poor to have a sauna. Quite often a young couple would build a sauna and live in it while their home was being built. Styles of construction changed, though only slightly. Today's home sauna is basically the same as those a hundred years old. The *savu sauna,* or smoke sauna, the precursor of modern accommodations, could easily be recognized today for what it was.

The savu sauna was, of course, built of logs, which were tightly chinked so that no heat could escape. The most important item it contained was the fireplace, a crude pile of stone which furnished the heat by which the steam for bathing was produced. It had no means of venting smoke, not even a hole in the roof in most cases, though in later times there was the added refinement of a trapdoor to release smoke when it got too bad. (Perhaps this was introduced because of un- explained deaths in the sauna, which we now know could have been caused by unburned wood and charcoal producing carbon monoxide gas when steam was formed in water being thrown on the rocks.) The only furnishings it needed were benches for the bathers and a barrel for the water.

Early in the day, the sauna fire would be built, usually by the wife or daughter, although in later times a young boy was assigned the duty, and frequently in America the hus- band would perform the chore. Water was carried in pails to fill the barrel, and the fire stoked again and again. As the day wore on, the water would get hot, and the rocks even more so. The *Kalevala* explains how the young daughter-in-law should make the preparations, even to the details of picking twigs of birch to make switches and inviting her father-in- law to use it first. She would issue her invitation after the fire had been allowed to die down to coals, the acrid wood smoke dissipated through the smoke slot, and fresh cold water brought.

Oddly enough, the bathers did not turn black from their exposure in the smoke-laden building. There was something in the combining of smoke and steam which seemed to glaze the benches, though the unwary who touched the ceiling might be rewarded with a soot-stained hand. The *vihta* (bouquet of leafy boughs) was dipped in water and the drops allowed to sizzle on the rocks before it was used to switch the body lightly and stimulate circulation. A clean, glowing skin was the result of even this primitive bath.

In any case, the savu sauna is an experience of a different order from that of a modern sauna. We can say "is" because some fortunate Finns often enjoy the use of it. Today you can still find Finns who relish the distinctive smell and eye-smarting feel of an old savu sauna. Fragrant from long years of usage, the smoke smell has permeated every timber. The walls are black with the layers of soot, which lies like lacquer on the benches. You would fear that it would be impossible to emerge from such a dungeonlike place feeling or looking clean, but such is not the case. The vihta dipped in water and laid on the rocks to sizzle give off an aromatic steam that is sweet and pungent at the same time. There are a few old savu saunas in the outlands, and the experience is not one to be missed.

A present-day sauna is much more sophisticated. Generally the interior displays light, bright wood such as birch or poplar, though the building itself may be made of pine logs. Redwood is never used in Finland. The heat is furnished by a wood stove, and on top of the stove, on a flat surface or in a metal cage, are closely piled rocks. They're not just any old rocks. A Finn seeks sauna rocks in swirling rivers, because a rock that has not withstood the test of long water washing may explode when heated. (Relax! There is no record of any death in Finland from flying sauna rocks.) The room contains wooden benches built like bleachers in stairstep fashion with gaps to let water drip through. There's a drain in the floor, a chimney, and barrels for water and pails for washing. It's customary for the water to be heated by passing it through the firebox in pipes.

The ritual is the same as that practiced for centuries. A fire is built early enough to allow the room to be saturated with heat. Heating the sauna shouldn't be hurried. A quick fire may warm the air, but the radiant heat from the walls is missing. Barrels are filled, the fire is fed at regular intervals, and the sauna is ready. The vihta, the dipper, the towels and soap are laid out, and the eager bathers take their turns.

A sauna will usually accommodate several people (except for the electrically heated saunas in private homes in the United States, which must be small to conserve energy). It's customary to bathe with members of your own sex or with your spouse. Mixed bathing of adults, never.

Except in such places as motels, Finns jeer at the idea of wearing bathing suits in the sauna. They say it is like washing your feet with your socks on.

Bathers remove their clothing in the anteroom, or dressing room. Then they disperse themselves on the benches in the inner room, where the *kiuas* (sauna stove) is doing its job. Only a sissy would bring a towel to sit upon, though it's permissible to use your washcloth to breathe through, and if your hair is damp or wrapped in a towel, it is much less likely to frizzle. Among Finns, the ability to climb up on the top bench and remain there while clouds of steam swirl around you is much prized as a means of separating the men from the boys, or weeding out those who are short of sisu.

The first period of the sauna is spent in absorbing the heat in every part of the body. Oddly enough, the sensation is one of comfort and languor, a complete relaxation of the body as the heat penetrates the tissues. The bather sits quietly and feels as if he is adrift on a cloud. Make no mistake, troubles lose their importance in the sauna. There is something in the heating of the blood that wipes out the frustrations and irritations of the day. Conversation is permissible, but it is never hilarious or controversial.

Presently it is time for a more active ritual. Water is dipped from the hot water barrel, either with the whisks or a dipper, and sprinkled on the rocks. Steam bursts forth in a hissing cloud, sometimes causing a rapid exodus of the neophytes from the top bench, and the bather's body becomes bathed in sweat. Here, again, the feeling is one of well-being.

Hardy bathers may repeat the process several times. As the steam wafts over the body, it sweats and impurities released through the skin are rinsed away. Incidentally, if you have encountered sauna-goers who regard it as an occasion for horseplay, dousing the kiuas so that bathers must crawl out of the room on hands and knees, they are ignorant louts who know less about the sauna than you, and rude besides.

Washing with soap and water is next. Each bather receives a pail of water, adjusted to the temperature he prefers. If the host or hostess is present with the bathers, it is customary for him or her to "make the water" for the guests. This step may also be skipped when the sauna is built beside a lake, which is where a Finn will put it if it's humanly possible.

At this point the bathers burst from the steam room and dash down to the lake, diving in immediately. It is a sight to make the stranger quail and the uninitiated marvel, as lobster-pink bodies hurtle down the slope and leap without pause into the water. In the wintertime, they may descend more decorously down a ladder into the water through a hole in the ice or roll about in the powdery snow. Non-Finns find this hard to believe, but once experienced, it's easy to understand.

Sauna-goers explain it this way. When your body is thoroughly heated in the sauna, the coldness of the water feels good. Presently the crisp bite of the cold water seeps into your bones, and you return to the heat of the sauna, which then feels good. Strangely enough, the sauna doesn't seem nearly so hot upon returning to it after a trip into the water.

Not everyone uses the vihta, but for old-time Finns it is indispensable. When the body is perspiring, a light switching all over with the supple branches stimulates in some mysterious way, causing a tingling, pleasurable sensation.

And oh, the feeling of cleanliness within and without, the feeling of relaxation and confidence and content!

Private saunas are becoming ever more luxurious. Now they frequently encompass three rooms. First is the dressing room, which is equipped with towels, places for hanging clothes, a mirror, and cosmetics. A middle room serves as a cooling room; it has long covered benches for relaxing and cooling, a shower, and a refrigerator stocked with cold beer and other refreshments. Some saunas have even a porch for later relaxing. But the heart of the building is the inner room with the kiuas.

The brave or curious tourist may present himself at one of the many public saunas, intending to experience this much-discussed pleasure. He should go with a group lest his first unwary experience be his last.

More than likely he will be met by an august personage: a woman of middle years and imposing size, intimidatingly dignified and serious. She is the bath maid, whose business it is to see that he is well scrubbed and well pummeled. She shoves him from compartment to compartment, and there is no way he can escape her ministrations.

It is of no use for the unwary male to cower shyly or show timidity. This impassive individual will not let her victim escape any part of the prescribed ritual. Modesty is no deterrent, and she has not been selected for her gentleness or delicacy.

Temperatures in the sauna vary. Eighty degrees celsius (176 degrees Fahrenheit) is a comfortable temperature. Yes, comfortable. The dry heat causes no disagreeable sensation of wilting, but your hair may become almost too hot to touch and women with earrings had better remove them to avoid burns.

The purpose of the sauna is not to boil you alive, though people often endure temperatures of 100 degrees Celsius

(212 degrees Fahrenheit—that's boiling!) with no ill effects. But this is generally merely to see how it feels. Most devotees prefer a somewhat lower temperature.

Sauna etiquette? It's informal, of course. (Try to be dignified in your birthday suit.) However, oldsters have certain feelings about proper conduct. It's not a place for exuberance or horseplay. It's even frowned upon to whistle. As it happens, only a few misguided jokesters need such guidance. Something about the relaxing heat curbs loud laughter or hilarity. The sauna, says one writer, is holy, like a church.

The importance of the sauna is not hard to understand. It is mystifying, however, that other nations did not immediately see its utility and adopt it. Even today, in most of the world a sauna is a luxury and a status symbol rather than a necessity.

A Finn would consider this a very upside-down view of the matter. He would regard a sauna as an essential part of his life-style. And why not? Think about what the sauna is.

It is a bathhouse. Though historic, it offers an especially efficient method of maintaining one's personal hygiene since the skin is cleansed from the inside out. People in the northern regions of the world, with the exception of the Finns, were once notorious for their lack of personal hygiene, and who can blame them? Perhaps this worked to their advantage in natural selection—only the hardiest could endure the threat of asphyxiation from a neighbor who simply added another layer of clothing when one layer got dirty or the weather grew colder.

In a cold climate, the sauna provides the most enjoyable way of cleansing the body. Upon stepping out of a tub in a chilly room, one hardly feels pleasure. But the stored heat in the body from a sauna is so great that even in winter, after that plunge in the lake or roll in the snow, the bather can stroll slowly back up the hill from the sauna to the house, stark naked. In fact it's the most comfortable way to proceed, and some time must be spent cooling off even before that. This is not odd at all. Finns have demonstrated that you can cook an egg in the sauna, just holding it in your hand.

The Finnish addiction to cleanliness probably came about because using the sauna was such an enjoyable rite. Today it has reached the status of an entertainment in many areas, where a Finn with a fine, large sauna may ask a friend, "Come on over to sauna," instead of "Come for a drink." More than likely, the drink will be there also, but the high point of the evening will be a session in the steam, uncurling the mind and feeling at peace with the world. Those incredible Finns! Who else would entertain their friends by offering them a bath?

The sauna is also physically and emotionally therapeutic. It's a special comfort to the athlete or laborer whose muscles are sore, since it removes stiffness from unaccustomed exertion. As a heat treatment for joint or muscle pain, it's gently and wonderfully effective.

The feeling after a sauna is one of euphoria. The mind is at peace, through some strange spiritual benefit from the all-encompassing warmth. The tired business man or woman feels worries melt away. It's evident that the old Greeks and Romans weren't the only ones who admired a sound mind in a sound body. In providing a sauna, the Finn is holding out a wholesome, mind-soothing, health-restoring ritual.

In a small way the sauna was the equivalent of the psychiatrist's couch. Anyone who has experienced it can testify to the value of a lazy session lying on the top bench, with heat permeating all the cells of the body. A comfortable feeling of lassitude steals over one, and a tranquil equanimity puts troubles in a different perspective. The fact that we speak of

Finns as stolid points to the probability that the sauna has conditioned them not to be excitable.

It's been touted by spas as a reducing treatment, which it is not, and a beauty treatment, which it well may be, since clean, healthy skin and hair are basic to any beauty ritual. A woman, says one authority, is most beautiful after her sauna. Possibly he meant a couple of hours after, because she is likely to be red faced and frizzy haired as she emerges from the sauna. Still, it adds a glow to the spirit as well as to the complexion, and the skins of the oft-bathed Finnish girls are almost luminously clear. Several of them have been beauty queens, and at least one Miss Universe was Finnish.

It induces vigor, they tell you, and endurance. A sauna quickens circulation and rids the body of toxins. As for endurance, there is the oft-told story of Eino and Toivo (two Finns, the equivalent of Pat and Mike) being captured by cannibals and popped into the pot. The hungry chief waited with fork in hand until such time as he judged them to have been sufficiently tenderized and then removed the cover. From the depths of the steam within came a querulous voice raised in complaint: "Vere's da cedar boughs?"

At times when virulent infections wreaked their havoc upon the populace, it became the hospital. Many a Finn has been born in the sauna, where heat had rendered the atmosphere nearly sterile, and water was at hand. In its rooms the old medicine women performed the rite of "cupping," or drawing blood to give health to the sick. Although bleeding is a treatment that for the most part went out with the powdered wig, Finnish cupping women performed their treatments in the twentieth century, even in America.

Their preoccupation with the body has led some people to think of Finns as sexually permissive, as their neighbors, the Swedes and Norwegians, are thought to be. Such people are apt to be disappointed. True, nudity is no novelty to Finns—

small children usually bathe with their parents—but adult Finns are no more lax in their morals than any other modern people. It does happen, however, that this utterly matter-of-fact acceptance of the human body as something everybody has, and of no particular glamour, has resulted in some amusing (and to the victim, upsetting) contretemps.

Recently, a young American woman, who was bathing Finnish-style for the first time at the lakeside sauna of her huband's Finnish cousin, was rendered utterly apoplectic when her host, arriving home after his guests and wishing to welcome his cousin without delay, flung open the door of the sauna and rushed in. To her horror, he insisted on shaking hands with her husband, speaking joyful words of greeting while she cowered in a corner, screening herself most inadequately with her hands. The aftershock came when he extended the same courtesy to her, and since she had only two hands, it left her feeling hopelessly mortified. Completely unaware of any embarrassment, her host welcomed her sincerely. She, however, was unable to stop blushing for the rest of her visit and never forgave him.

Now that most motels and apartment complexes in the United States include a sauna in their building plans, there are few Americans who cannot boast of having experienced its benefits. In the fanciest of private homes it is a status symbol as well as a health and beauty treatment. Unquestionably the sauna has become an amenity of the elegant life, and is no longer a simple means of keeping clean. Finally we have discovered that the Finns were right all along.

It is no wonder that the sauna habit has been joyfully seized upon and spread throughout all the world. The wonder is that it took so long.

The start of the Annual Finlandia Ski Race in Hämeenlinna.

CHAPTER 14

THE CHALLENGE IS PERSONAL

LIFE IS SUCH A SERIOUS MATTER to the Finnish people that they work hard even when they are playing. Sport to the Finn does not mean spending Sunday afternoon in front of a television set with a beer in hand, watching a couple of dozen behemoths commit mayhem on one another. No, his or her choice is a sport that requires individual effort, not team strength, and tests the skill and stamina of each performer. As a nation we have recently discovered jogging, but the Finns have been at it for a long time. The result of this interest in physical activity is that Finns as a group are exceptionally fit.

If you ask a Finn what his or her favorite sport is, it's apt to begin with an *S*: swimming, skiing, skating, soccer, or sailing. All of these are possible to any Finn because there is lots of room for open-air pursuits, and there are glimmering waterways within reach of everyone.

Skiing is probably the Finns' first love. After all, it was their invention, though it's popular wherever there's snow. Skiing is available anywhere in Finland in winter, and in the northern sector the snow comes in October.

The Finns have been skiing for so long that it's next to impossible to say when they began. Some skis have been found that are more than 3700 years old, which puts them so far back in the dark that we don't know much about those who used them. The old-timers who wagged their heads at the primitive lives of the newly discovered Finns made much of their ability to get around on their flat boards and even outrun animals. There are fourteen-foot skis in a Finnish museum which must have been worn by somebody. Maybe it was our old friend Lemminkäinen because the *Kalevala* mentions that he took time off from chasing girls to "ski down" the Demon's elk.

Skiing has changed a lot, particularly in recent years, with emphasis on lighter equipment for speed. A racing ski is likely to be slender and springy, not at all like some we see in photographs of skiing parties fifty years ago—the skis are nine feet long and eight inches wide! Actually, these would do very well for transportation in open areas, since they slide across the top of loose drifts. But in a wooded area, or in places where a trail turns sharply, they are hopelessly clumsy.

Throughout the winter almost every community has its own weekly ski competitions, and everyone is expected to take part. In the Kemi competition, a number of eighty-year-olds compete. For the expert, there are world class competitions at Lahti and Kuopio; and for the traditionalist, the Oulu Tervakilpailu ("tar race") is the oldest skiing competition in the world. In Hämeenlinna about seven thousand skiers from twenty countries showed up to compete in the Finlandia Ski Race of 1980.

Americans got a fascinating glimpse of Finland's athletic prowess in the 1980 Winter Olympics, when Finland's team marched in, resplendent in the blue and white of their national colors. The flag was borne by Juha Mieto, their cross-country ski star. When the competition ended, Finland had snared nine medals—a gold, five silver, and three bronze. Fans will long remember that the Finnish hockey team almost won against the Russians and the narrow margin by which they lost to the United States.

In their traditional events, their competitors were right up front. Juho Mieto came home with a silver medal in the cross-country contest, only the length of a short pencil behind the gold medal winner in a nine-mile course. In the ninety-meter ski jumping, Jouko Toermaenen's incredible floating leap secured the gold, with his teammate Jari Puikkonen a close third, winning the bronze. Women's cross-country was dominated by Finland, too. Hilda Riihivouri and Helena Takalo finished a bare ten seconds apart for the silver and bronze.

In World War II the Finns dazzled the world with their mobile, quick-striking force of ski troops, and in no time at all the United States had units training in Colorado for the same type of warfare. (Being trained, one might add, by Nordics.)

When the Japanese felt the need of a little expert assistance to teach cross-country skiing to their athletes, they called on a Finn, Erik Pihkala. He was so proficient at sixty years of age that the Italians nicknamed him the "Astronaut of the Snow." Just for fun, Pihkala skiied for more than a month in Greenland, with the thermometer at -40 degrees.* He also skiied over the Lapland fells to Norway and Sweden on what is known as the Path of Death. This trip is unusually rigorous, but it's not uncommon for a ski tour to cover five hundred to a thousand miles. That's serious.

Not all Finns insist on being that proficient. It's a sport for the individual, and if he or she is satisfied with the performance, that's enough. It's a do-it-yourself sport, and you are free to enjoy it in your own way.

The story is told of a visitor who thought it looked like so much fun, he would like to try it. As he stepped into his skis,

---

* It is a curious fact that -40 degrees Celsius and -40 degrees Fahrenheit are equal.

a helpful Finn pointed out, "You are putting your skis on backwards." The novice glared.

"How the hell do you know which way I'm going?"

Downhill skiing, an Alpine import, is likewise popular, but the skill required keeps it from being the widely practiced sport that cross-country skiing is. Still, within the reach of everyone, there are ski hills which allow varying degrees of proficiency. For a spectator, the greatest thrill is watching the experts zoom down the precipitous slopes of the jumps at Kuopio or Lahti and take off like a bird to land in a glide a hundred feet away.

The highest hills of Finland are in the northern sector. Elsewhere, the Finns have improved on nature by building towers, the better to break their necks.

Hockey is Finland's most important winter game, and great enthusiasm follows Finnish hockey teams as they perform brilliantly at home and gracefully overwhelm our American teams on tour. Skating doesn't generate nearly the enthusiasm that skiing and hockey do. Make no mistake, there are Finns in this sport who are tough competitors, both in speed skating and figure skating, but they are fewer in number and lack the impact that Finland's skiers and hockey players have.

In winter as in summer the Finns take to their lakes in boats. Their ice boats have a light framework, runners, and a sail, and breathtaking speeds may be attained. Breathtaking close calls and accidents are also included. Ice boating is not for the timid, but if you are well padded or don't mind risking your teeth and bones, it's exhilarating.

As one looks out over a snow-covered lake, it is not unusual to see it dotted with people squatting on camp chairs or buckets, gazing prayerfully at small holes in the ice and holding an eighteen-inch rod in their hands. These are the ice fishermen, the men and women who didn't get all their fishing done in summer. It's a sport of its own, and there are fishing contests in the late winter. The real enthusiasts go from contest to contest, winning attractive prizes. Sometimes the trappings get quite elaborate, with huts, heaters, and padded chairs, and beer buried in a handy snowbank. Skill and patience are the chief requirements, for the fish are alert to noises and shadows on the ice above them. One family in the lake country—Maire Tahvanainen and her children—make it a way of life, and not just because they like to eat pike and perch.

For ice fishing, you have to disguise yourself as the Abominable Snowman, wearing heavy garments to keep from freezing in the long, still hours of waiting by the hole in a biting wind. In winter less hardy lake lovers may prefer car races on the ice, a slippery pastime that has been around since the early 1930s. For this, the snow must be plowed from the lake surface in a complicated track of whirls and curves. To the spectator, it may not look difficult, but the drivers who guide cars sliding smoothly at high speed must have nerve, skill, and timing. As for equipment, the same car that hauled the family to see Grandma is equipped with studded tires and becomes the contest vehicle. So many take part that barely a foot is allowed between competing cars at the starting line. It may be crazy but it's fun and not as lethal as it may sound, although collisions are part of the game. There are four thousand licensed racing drivers, which means that one out of each thousand persons in Finland holds a license.

All good things must come to an end, and even in Lapland the snow melts sometime. Soon after the ice is out, the season for water sports begins. There is no excuse for a Finnish child being unable to swim, and there are very few indeed who don't take to the water at every opportunity. A swim is especially enjoyable if combined with a sauna.

Proficiency in this sport is tested, and the swimmer progresses through several levels of skill. Being able to swim is important to the honor of your country! Every year, the Nordic nations compete to see which of the four countries has the most people who can pass a swimming test. The standards are the same for everyone, and everyone is tested. Each nation's score is computed on the basis of what percentage of the population can swim. Of course, there are always a few timid souls who spoil the national record. Zealous competitors search them out and see to it that their next performance is better.

Swimming is important, and it's not only because it's fun and a means of keeping fit. So many other popular Finnish sports involve water that without swimming instruction, there would be a danger of citizens drowning in great numbers before they were old enough to vote.

There is sailing, for instance. Finland has had a yacht club since 1861 and still builds beautiful pleasure craft.

For the more daring, shooting the rapids is now a favorite sport. There is plenty of fast water in Finland. One river, the Imatra, is so powerful that it has been said, "No one crosses the Imatra." (One can do so now, however; a bridge spans it.) If you are bored with life, you can shoot the rapids in a kayak or canoe at any number of exciting spots—Rukatunturi is especially well known. It's not an entertainment for the fainthearted at any time, and the Emajoki, with its eleven rapids in eleven miles, is a test of skill and courage guaranteed to raise the hair on your neck.

Anyone can get to water. There are plenty of public beaches, and they are attractive, with or without the beautiful Finnish girls who decorate them. There's no littering or trash scattered about, for the Finns are proud of their country, and their national habits of neatness and self-discipline work to make them keep their parks clean.

With all the area of forest and water, a weekend camping trip is a convenient possibility, and hiking trails and boating excursions abound. Accustomed though they are to natural beauty all around them, the Finns are especially fond of the lake district to the west of Lahti, where shimmering Lake Saimaa is part of a wandering waterway of serene loveliness and peace.

Lakes and woods mean fishing and hunting, and these sports offer trophies that make the eyes of the ardent angler or hunter pop. Salmon attract fishermen from all of Europe, and the gigantic trout is famous. Spearing fish at night is especially exciting. Sitting in the bow of a small boat, with a three-pronged spear in one hand and a powerful torch in the other, the sportsman watches for the quicksilver quarry. One jab, and he either has his dinner or has alerted the wary fish. Along with ice fishing, this gives a fisherman a chance to tell lies all year round.

The wild animals of Finland's early history still inhabit the forests. Bears and wolves are not so numerous as they were in the days when there were fewer people, but they are there. The chief game animal is the elk. American tourists are apt to look at this animal and exclaim, "That's a moose!" The animals do look very much alike. The moose, which also goes by the name of American elk, is a member of the same species.

The likeliest place to see this broad-antlered beast is around Helsinki, and they are so numerous in early summer that there are even road signs to warn drivers. In a collision with the huge animal, no one wins, though more elk than people are killed in this manner.

Elk, like everyone else in Finland, must know how to read. Although they have been seen outside Parliament House, near the post office, admiring the Mannerheim Memorial, and even by Finlandia Hall, they make themselves scarce during the hunting season.

Finland has about seventy thousand of these ungainly looking creatures and permits about seventeen thousand to be taken each year. The season is from October to December. The game is not wasted. Though the hunter may keep the trophy, the meat and hide belong to the landowner. Those who long for a taste will find elk on the menu in many restaurants. It's delicious—rather like lean beef.

For a genuine spectator sport, in which only the highly skilled participate, there are the loggers' competitions. Most of them take place in North Karelia and are part of ethnic festivals in which old customs have been revived. Individuals compete in events that test skills to the utmost. The most exciting is the death-defying attempt of each logger to shoot the dangerous falls by riding on a log with only a pole for balance. There are famous champions and crowd favorites, though anyone may compete if he really wants to.

With all this going on, it's surprising that Finns have time for any other game, but they do. A favorite is called "pesä pällo." Try pronouncing it, and you will see that it sounds like "baseball." It looks a little bit like baseball, too, but Babe Ruth would never recognize it. In the Finnish version, the catcher pitches, and if the batter should hit a home run, he's out. The Finns also play football, but professional teams are unknown.

Mention Finns in sport, and somebody is sure to speak of running. An Icelandic saga of 1020 reports on a runner called Finn the Little, who was so fleet that no horse could overtake him. And it must have been a national sport of some importance—the Finnish language has twenty words for running.

Long distance running in modern times has had the Finns out front since the days of Paavo Nurmi, who earned the name "Flying Finn" from his Olympic victory in 1924. An iron man, he won the 1500-meter and 5000-meter races within an hour, exerting incredible stamina and merciless willpower. In three months he took part in forty-five races, winning all but one. Having won nine Olympic medals and holding twenty world records, he has to be considered the greatest runner the world has ever known. Sports fans outside of Finland goggled when they heard that Nurmi ate black bread and fish and took "Finn baths."

The names of Finnish athletes have cropped up regularly on the Olympic lists since Finland first entered the Olympic games in 1906 and had four winners. President Urho Kekkonen was an Olympic high jump champion, and no doubt his athletic self-discipline helps him in his role today. The present standard-bearer in long distance running is the incomparable Lasse Viren. With his powerful flying step he swept the gold in both the 1972 and 1976 Olympics. Although he ran gallantly in the 1980 Moscow games, taking the lead several times, it was his teammate Kaario Maaninka who took the silver medal in the 10,000-meter and the bronze in the 5000-meter race.

There are no professional athletes in Finland. Juha Väätainen taught school when he wasn't running. Nurmi was of working-class parents and held his first job as an errand boy when he was only twelve. Finnish athletes are amateurs in the basic meaning of the word. They receive no scholarships, sinecures, or subsidies. Each performs for the honor of Finland until a younger competitor edges him or her out.

Participation and competition rather than international glory is the name of the game in Finland. Everyone tries, not just the famous few whose shoes line the shelves of the Helsinki Sports Museum.

School days. Except for the map on the wall, this classroom in Espoo could be anywhere in Europe where blond heads predominate.

CHAPTER 15

OUT OF THEIR MINDS

WITH ALL THE EMPHASIS on brawn, we might think that the Finns neglect their brains. Not a bit. The creative minds of the Finns are recognized as among their greatest resources, and they're not about to let them be lost by default. To the citizens of Finland, education is not a privilege, it is a duty. This philosophy goes back to an old church law of 1686 that forbade marriage to anyone who couldn't read, thereby forcing those who wanted to live happily ever after to get some schooling.

The Finns regard education as the keystone of their democracy, and so they put their money on it. A whopping 18 percent of the national budget is allocated for education. This is the largest single slice of a pie that gives 5 percent to defense and administration, 8 percent to health, and 6.9 percent to housing. Small wonder, then, that the literacy rate in Finland in 1978 was 99 percent. Almost half of the allotment is spent on elementary education. It is directed by the Ministry of Education, which furnishes ideas and guidelines, but supervision of the schools is a local affair.

The goals of education, as the Finns see it, are to insure equal opportunity for all citizens and to improve the quality of life. To these ends, they have frequently revised their educational system. The latest reform, now fully implemented, puts their faith in what is called *peruskoulu,* a basic or comprehensive school system.

The new comprehensive system replaces one in which students progressed through a series of schools known as *kansakoulu* ("elementary"), *oppikoulu* ("learning"), *keskikoulu* ("middle"), and *lukio* ("senior high") on different tracks according to their abilities and career choices. In the new approach there is an emphasis on the personality development of each child. The purpose of the school is to enrich living for the individual and to provide, if possible, needed marketable skills. Within this guideline a system of nine years' education that is fundamentally the same for everyone has been set up and vocational schools established. The trend is to secure a vocational education for each young person before he or she enters the labor market, along with a broad, basic liberal education.

The reform was begun in northern Finland, and gradually introduced throughout the country. The small village of Lieksa, located near the Soviet border, was one of the pioneers, drawing its student body from a land area of more than 1500 square miles (4100 square kilometers). The last area to install the new system was the urban capital, Helsinki.

School is not only compulsory, it is free. Books are free, paper is free, meals are free. Medical care, dental care, clothing, and transportation are provided wherever needed. The money for all of this comes mostly from the state, though local authorities bear a small part of the expense.

Compulsory attendance begins at age seven. Actually, the child enters the educational system as early as five or six in many cases through day-care centers. Nearly half of Finland's children are now included in the public day-care system. Besides that, a small group, about 2 percent of the six-year-olds, has been admitted to the comprehensive school. This has led to the suggestion that compulsory education begin at age six, since almost one-sixth of the children of that age are not enrolled in any kind of preschool activity.

Students may leave school at sixteen, if they wish, but in that time they have had nine years of thorough education.

The prescribed subjects at the first grade level are religion, mathematics, environmental studies, music, art, handicrafts, and either Finnish or Swedish, whichever is the student's native language.

Second grade is much the same. Physical education doesn't come into the picture until grade three. At that time a second language is added (most probably Swedish or Finnish, but frequently English), along with natural history and geography. The fifth graders have history, civics, and social studies added to their curriculum.

The school day begins at eight o'clock in the morning and lasts until three in the afternoon, Monday through Friday, mid-August through May. The beginner puts in a twenty-one hour week. This is gradually extended to thirty hours for the student of junior high school age. The long Christmas vacation divides the school year handily into two terms, with a three-month summer holiday and (you won't believe this) a week's ski vacation in winter.

Perhaps the most striking feature of Finnish education is the insistence on foreign languages for the whole population. Not one, but two languages are introduced at the lower level. Many students begin their study of English, Russian, French, or German in third grade. In seventh grade an additional foreign language is added. This reflects an awareness that in a small country where trade is a lifeline, knowledge of foreign languages is paramount. Finland and Iceland are the only nations in the world which teach two foreign languages to the entire populace.

Once the lower six grades are completed, the students move up to the second level of comprehensive school. In what we would call seventh grade, they begin to choose their subjects according to personal interests. A few wrong guesses are allowed. If Maija or Marku decides that the subject elected is not a good choice after all, it's perfectly all right to switch, in mid-term if necessary.

Besides the foreign language, domestic science and physics or chemistry are added to the course load. Technical and commercial courses are optional, as are forestry, horticulture, and another foreign language. Although mathematics is required, it is offered as either a short course or a long one. Religion also remains a part of the curriculum.

When they finish comprehensive school, the students have two options: to continue onward and upward in the upper secondary school (equivalent to senior high school) or to opt for the vocational school. Those who choose the upper secondary school will be preparing for admission to one of the institutions of higher learning. We who assume that anyone may go to high school are surprised to learn that entrance into Finland's upper secondary school is selective. Only those who have finished comprehensive school with an acceptable grade point average are eligible. Then, too, they must have completed at least the intermediate level of the optional courses.

Obviously, when students take the same basic courses in comprehensive school, there will be differences in how well they do and how much they learn. Because of this, the upper level of the comprehensive school is planned to offer the widest possible diversification. Thus it serves as a preparatory school for upper secondary education, and is still a springboard for vocational school.

The upper secondary school corresponds roughly with the accelerated courses in our senior high schools. In a five-day week the student puts in about thirty-five hours and takes several required subjects, including religion. Psychology, philosophy, a third foreign language, and other optional courses allow for special interests. At the end of three years comes the day of reckoning in the form of the matriculation examination, which will decide whether or not the student may enter an institution of higher learning. It is not quite the equivalent of the dreaded *ylioppilastutkinto* of byegone days, when failure meant utter disgrace. This examination, however, as well as an upper secondary school certificate, is required to open the doors of a university. And even then, acceptance is not guaranteed. Because of a shortage of openings, less than half of those who have finished upper secondary school will enter the halls of higher education. It behooves those aspiring to such a future to make sure of a good grade-point average as well as a high score on the examination.

Parallel with the upper secondary school is the vocational school. This also requires a comprehensive school certificate, but its goal is to prepare the student directly for the job market. At the same time, students completing this training are able to continue their education if they choose.

Vocational education was expanded after World War II because of the obvious immediate need for trained workers when the Finns were struggling to meet Soviet reparations. Reorganization of the strictly practical nature of these schools has been a continuing process ever since. At present, along with the vocational courses, general subjects are taught to provide eligibility for higher education at vocational institutes as well as universities. To make sure that this goal becomes an actuality, a certain number of openings in higher education are reserved for those who complete vocational school.

Another concept aimed at furthering the students' chances for continued education is the formation of basic lines. These lines of training are broader than any given job, so that the twenty-four fields of study encompass a total of ten times that number of trained vocations. The list of broad categories is surprising; agriculture (with horticulture and dairying considered separate), textiles, automobiles and transport, mechanical engineering, electrical engineering, chemical engineering, health care, and merchant marine are all considered basic lines of study. In addition, there are twenty other lines requiring specialized study. The system is designed to minimize overlapping while broadening vocational skills.

Selection for both upper secondary schools and vocational schools is a regional process, so that all students have the same opportunities wherever they live. Career counseling begins early, and school authorities and labor organizations cooperate to direct students toward the best opportunities. The state helps to equalize matters further by offering grants and loans to students and subsidizing operating costs.

The underlying aim of vocational education is to meet the needs of the job market while occupying young people until they reach employable age. Those who leave comprehensive school at the age of sixteen are not likely to enter the ranks of wage earners with any degree of success, and a floating population of unemployed teenagers is hardly desirable. At the same time, an attempt is made to correlate the openings in vocational school with the jobs actually available so that a trained worker finds a market for his or her skills.

But it must never be thought that a young person is shunted irrevocably into one path or another. Those who complete vocational school are not destined merely to fill the demand for a labor force. They have received a general education that includes national languages, mathematics, sciences, physical education, health, art, and (hang onto your hat) environmental appreciation. They are ready for higher education if they choose to go on.

Again there is a double track before them: the high-level vocational institute or the university.

The vocational institute aims at preparing students for high level positions, primarily in management and planning. A vocational course at institute level may take as long as four years and offer some 650 different courses.

The eighteen university-level institutions in Finland put higher education within reach of anyone. The oldest of these, established at Turku in 1640, is hoary with tradition. The newest is the University of Lapland, established at Rovaniemi in 1979. Oulu, Kuopio, Joensuu, Tampere, Lapeenranta, and Jväskylä all have universities as well, but the University of Helsinki is the giant, having nearly one-third of all the students.

Thirteen thousand new hopefuls join the university system each year, and a total of eighty thousand (about 17 percent of the eligible age group) is enrolled. About half of the university student population is female. More than half the students are occupied with the humanities: social science, law, business and education. Another quarter study natural science, including agriculture and forestry. Engineering accounts for another 16 percent, while 8 percent are in medicine.

A university education is within reach of any ambitious Finn, if he or she has the brains. Nearly all the expense is borne by the state. Even the privately owned institutions are state funded. In 1980, the Sibelius Academy, the only one in recent years to charge tuition (and that infinitesimal, by modern standards), became a state institution. No one can give "lack of money" as a reason for lack of learning.

Earning a degree that is the equivalent of a bachelor of arts takes four to six years. The reward is the formidable title of *humanististentieteden kandidaatii*. *Maisteri* ("master's") follows kandidaatti. Advanced degrees confer such titles as

lisensiaatti ("licensed practitioner") and *tohtori* ("doctor").
Licensed practitioners are those who have completed graduate
studies, and frequently a thesis as well, while the doctor's
degree implies original research and the observing and
solving of problems.

School is never over for the Finn who wants to go on. The
adult education program is so extensive and far reaching
that it doesn't fit into any one general description.

The core of it is the folk school system. This idea was born
in Denmark more than a hundred years ago, as a practical
alternative to the classical education of the day. Like the
Danes, the Finns reasoned that there was another field of
learning, equally important, for young people with no
professional leanings who wanted to enrich their lives.
Emphasis was at first on Finnish national concerns: the
government, agricultural practices, and Finnish arts and
culture.

The folk school of today is a boarding school that
provides education in the arts, social and natural sciences,
and economics, as well as vocational skills. The minimum
age for admission is sixteen, and the focus is on personality
development. The graduation certificate doesn't qualify its
recipient for anything, but even so, in 1978 thirty thousand
students thought it was worth working for.

Civic and workers' institutes are the largest organizations
for adult education. They teach skills that are of practical
value in daily living, as well as leisure-time activities and
hobbies. Here, again, no qualifying degree or certificate is
conferred, but an institute may serve as a prerequisite for
higher education.

An ever-increasing number of people are members of
"study circles." The twenty thousand circles follow courses
of study chosen by the members themselves, under the wing
of a study center that guides but does not restrict. The state

furnishes the funds, provided that five people over fifteen years of age form a group to meet ten times for study of their chosen topic. The participants in 1978 numbered nearly two hundred thousand.

Evening schools for upper-secondary education are available to those adults who may have missed their chance first time around. They cover the same ground as the day schools. There are also courses for job retraining, which are available to those over twenty who are jobless, whose jobs are being phased out, or who need updated skills.

Education in Finland is seen as an ongoing, lifelong process. Generally it's an outgrowth of a need to be met. One example is the Tech Town (Institute of Technology) that grew up in Helsinki, as students set up classes and housing to bridge a gap in necessary training. *After* they arranged matters and got it going, they got official support.

Love of learning carries over into private life. Helsinki is celebrated for the Academic Book Store, which has the largest stock of foreign books to be found anywhere. The publishing industry thrives. Finland's Publishers Association has thirty-eight members, which produce 3800 titles a year. In 1978, 4.7 million Finns bought an astounding 24 million books.

Education is Finland's window on the world, and attitudes have changed since the old days in North Karelia, when a father was asked how his son had liked his first day of school. He'd gotten through it, the man said with relief, "Though it was tough on the little feller, not being able to smoke for all that time."

A musician in native dress plays the kantele, an ancient Finnish harp.

Chapter 16

FOLKWAYS

PROBLEM: If Eric XIV had managed to persuade Elizabeth I of England to marry him, as he tried to do, how would the Finns' folkways and character have been different?

It's interesting to speculate. So many of Finland's traditions are a result of its remote location, which kept the Finns out of mainstream European culture. Isolation nurtured a distinctly Finnish life-style that was a far cry from the mannered existence of the sophisticated English. Elizabeth would have had plenty of reason for her famous tantrums.

It's not surprising that Finland's stories of a thousand years ago are different from the ones found elsewhere in Europe. They share a pervasive melancholy tone, like a melody in a minor key. No jolly peasants or clever, ridiculous ruses, no moral lessons, no princes in disguise. No elves, fairies, or talking animals. In general the tales are about simple people encountering the stuff of mystery and dreams.

There is, for instance, the story of Star-Eyes, a foundling whose foster mother is so frightened by the child's second sight that she abandons her in Lapland. The foster father's attempt to rescue her is futile, and we pity the ignorant prejudice that condemns the foundling for powers she can't control. No trace of her is found, and the happiness of the family is ruined.

Bluebeard has his counterpart in the Sea God, but his

snoopy brides, instead of being decapitated, are immured in a keg of tar. Their rescue is accomplished not by the bravery of a swashbuckling male, but by the cleverness of his final wife. The Finns didn't expect an outsider to help them escape their fate. And the magic (surprise, surprise!) is mostly a matter of charms.

In spite of its great weight and richness, Finnish folk literature has made almost no impact on American readers. When you are tired of wicked stepmothers and greedy elves, try "Canute Whistlewinks," the story of a little boy who could call ducks, or "Lisalill," the tale of an enchanted girl-child.

The greatest collector of these tales was Zachris Topelius, son of a famous folklorist of the same name. Topelius was to Finland what Hans Christian Andersen was to Denmark, or the Grimm brothers to Germany. The folktales he collected, beginning in 1865, filled several volumes. It was an achievement precious to the Finns who, although they had no written language of their own until the nineteenth century, enjoyed a rich oral tradition.

The old Finnish charms that have been preserved for us are mostly incantations or exhortations. One might think that they were derived from work chants, to preserve the rhythm of the labor and make the job go easier. Perhaps in performing some feat allied with danger it was considered wise to invoke the help (or at least the good nature) of whatever deity might be in charge.

Besides the work charms, there were superstitions related to special gifts. Those who would rather find treasure than earn it might try sitting on a three-times-changed roof on Midsummer, keeping their eyes peeled for fire hovering over any handy swamp or lake. Mysterious blue flames meant that the spirits guarding treasure were burning off the mold and rust. But there was more to getting the treasure than seeing where it was. One had to dispose of fierce snakes, bulls, or other fearsome beasts that guarded it, and here again, one needed to utter the right charm.

It was possible to satisfy a craving to become invisible, too, by performing the proper ritual on Midsummer Night while observing the flowering of a fern. No one would attempt this nowadays since it is well known that the fern never flowers, but long ago believers betook themselves into dark swamps, placed themselves on a white sheet, and waited for the flowering. It took a good deal of courage and determination, since the place was guarded by demons and goblins of various sorts, all intent on mischief, and it's sad indeed that it must never have worked.

Today folklore is studied as enthusiastically as in the days of Topelius. The Society of Finnish Literature has published works on folk music that are conveniently in English if you aren't bilingual, as well as records. The society also brings forth scholarly studies of such topics as healers and their cures and the Finnish creation story. The World Conference of Folklorists even held a meeting in Helsinki a couple of years back.

The Finns' enthusiasm for their folktales is further shown by the fact that legendary heroes have continued to appear. In the early 1900s tales were told of Taulan-Antti, a backward backwoods villager. He and his brothers were loggers renowned both for their great strength and shy silence. One day as he was hauling a great sleigh-load of logs to the river, Taulan-Antti met a mail carrier. The mailman did not wish to move off the trail, and why should he? He had the right of way. Taulan-Antti resolved their differences by getting out of his seat, lifting the mailman's horse and sleigh, and placing them over the snowbank. Then he drove on, leaving the squealing mail carrier on the wrong side of the snowbank.

Taulan-Antti frequently appeared at church, where he lurked shyly out of doors and admired the horses and conveyances. Once he saw a bicycle and was greatly intrigued. In a matter of weeks, Taulan-Antti appeared at church riding a bicycle of his own. It was a handmade lumbering contraption with wooden wheels. But it worked!

Taulan-Antti's shyness points up what might be called a national trait—the fabled Finnish taciturnity. One story claims that an old settler in a remote fastness, on learning that he had a neighbor twenty miles away, drove him out. His reason? He didn't want to live in a crowded area. Finns protest that they don't say much because nobody understands them when they talk. Having a language different from anyone else's certainly would give one that handicap.

Sometimes this can be carried too far. There was once a Finn farmer who was plowing on a hot day while his mute fourteen-year-old son watched. There grew in the father a great desire for a cooling drink of buttermilk, and he made signs to the boy to fetch some from the house.

When the boy returned, the farmer seized the jug eagerly and began to drink until he was startled at hearing his son cry out, "Stop, Father! Leave some for me!"

The man nearly dropped the jug. "My son! You can speak!"

"Yes, Father."

"But why have you never spoken before?"

"There was never anything to talk about."

That's Finnish logic for you.

There's another story about a visitor who, in preparation for a night on the town with a Finnish friend, had taken pains to learn the Finnish equivalent of "Skål," which is "Kippis."

As the first drink was served, he exclaimed, "Kippis!" The Finn said nothing, and they drank.

Another drink appeared; the visitor again said heartily, "Kippis!" There was no response from his Finnish friend.

At the third drink, his "Kippis" was a little less hearty, and when the fourth came around, he said it almost timidly. At this, the Finn finally broke his silence:

"Talk, talk, talk! I thought we came here to drink."

Geographic isolation had its effect, too, on the national costume, called the *kansallispuku*. Deep down, the Finns are a colorful people, and formerly they expressed it in clothing that, alas, is rarely seen today. But "national" costume was a local matter. Even the neighboring province was a far journey, and not one you'd take often, being so busy with your own work. So in each area there was a distinctly different outfit for special occasions, and any stranger in your midst was spotted instantly.

Although each area had its own variations in costume, the general style was the same. Girls and women wore a skirt below the knee, full and gathered. It might be striped in Imatra and solid black with a red border elsewhere. Although most costumes were topped with a white apron, in some regions the apron was green. The blouse varied, too, though it was nearly always white, with full sleeves. Men's costume variations were equally prescribed: a gold knife belt, pointed shoes, or collarless shirt might proclaim the wearer's native region.

The festival dress was so important that no young woman wanted it splattered or creased on the way to the frolic. So another item, the "church box," came into being. It was a handsomely decorated chest in which a girl's best clothes (and probably those of other family members, too) were transported across the lake or along the muddy lane to the gathering place, to be donned there. Some of these old church boxes survive, mostly of wood artfully shaped and painted, as beautiful as the gay finery they held.

One item that was worn by every man was his knife, his *puukko,* which swung in an elaborate metal belt at a jaunty angle, much as Wild West gunslingers wore their weapons.

The puukko was more than a costume accessory. It was a weapon, a tool, and a utensil. Knife duels were common. The single-edged puukko was held near the point, with the duelist's forefinger extended along its back, and used in lightning thrusts and slashes. In those times an unscarred man must have been either a champion or a sissy.

It's not to be wondered at that the Finnish knife today is a craftsman's product, a thing of beauty. Among the most admired are those made in Kauhava. If you buy a knife made by J. Marttiini of Rovaniemi, you may have a choice ranging from a small tourist model to the giant Lapp *leuku* with its foot-long blade. All of them have a gently curved blade of stainless steel and a tooled leather case. Modern as the moment, this "old-fashioned" Finnish knife is everything the old Finns thought it was.

Innumerable other folk arts are being revived. The making of bobbin lace, ryijy rugs, *himmeli* (straw ornaments), fish nets, leather goods, weaving with yarn and birch strips, and wood carving are just a few.

Rauma's lace fair is a week-long affair held in July. Old lace is exhibited, and modern artisans with flying fingers demonstrate the way it is made. Folk music and local food specialties help to make the fair a high point in many a traveler's agenda.

There are other handicraft fairs, too. Perhaps the ones that best reflect the old culture are those held at Jan Karigarden's open air museum on the Åland Islands and in Turku's old wooden town. Craftsmen in traditional garb demonstrate their arts in the ancient streets, watched by the ghosts of their counterparts from centuries past. Visitors feel as if they are in a time warp as they watch carvers, weavers, and ironworkers absorbed in their crafts in age-old surroundings.

The revival of interest in folklore and crafts is welcome in a world where variations in folklife are fast disappearing. In the recent past the Finns delighted in being modern and dumped their old-fashioned ways when something better came along. Lately, however, a wave of nostalgia has swept over Finland. Throughout the summer traditional festivals are held, some of which are now world famous. The Ritvala Helka Festival re-creates a traditional procession of Helka maidens singing Helka hymns. In Naantali and Hangö, Sleepyhead Day begins with townspeople in their night-clothes joining the procession of revelers who awakened them and ends with a carnival. Karelian customs are revived in the Imatra festival, while the Kaustinen Folk Music Festival is a many-day spectacle of song and dance in colorful costume, which features a grand cavalcade of singers, musicians, and whirling dancers. The spirit of the festival so permeates the community of Kaustinen that the children, it is said, even cry to music.

This new reverence for the past makes shopping in Finland a joy to the visitor. Modern jewelry sits cheek by jowl with bronze medallions based on Finnish archeological finds. You can select a handwoven linen cloth or a gay nonwoven disposable one that is almost indistinguishable from the handcrafted article. Wood carvings of surpassing delicacy or robust humor are especially apropos, reflecting Finland's longtime preoccupation with this medium. Bas-reliefs commonly depict in caricature some of Finland's traditional activities, particularly sauna scenes in endless variation. Finns seem to regard their own doings with an eye for the ludicrous, making such things comic articles and art treasures at the same time. The visitor's problem is mainly that of having a suitcase that is large enough.

Students in Helsinki clamber up the statue of Havis Amanda to crown her with their caps on Vappu (May Day Eve).

Chapter 17

CELEBRATIONS

Mention the word "holiday" to a Finn, and you are apt to have started a lengthy conversation. When it comes to partying, the energetic Finns sail away with the prize and leave other celebrants panting in their wake. In fact, when there's a holiday, everything closes down so that the citizens may devote themselves to the serious business of enjoying themselves. On All Saints' Day, Independence Day, Christmas, and so on, they close half a day early to get into the spirit of it. Since the Lutheran church is a state church, days of special significance in the church calendar are legal holidays for believers and unbelievers alike. That includes Epiphany, Good Friday, and Easter Monday.

New Year's Eve comes first, of course, and the parties last through January 1. Then there is a breathing space before Kalevala Day, which is February 28. Bridging this time and for a period afterward, is the ski season, filled with winter sports competitions of world class at Lahti and Kuopio and community events all over.

Easter brings a change of pace. Some of the Easter traditions are holdovers from pagan times, when the season of new growth was hailed. Eggs, of course, figure prominently; some of them are the real thing, cooked and colored, while others are made of chocolate or marzipan. A special treat for the occasion is *mämmi,* a puddinglike concoction of rye flour, malt, and orange peel, sprinkled with sugar and swamped in cream. In bygone days it was baked and sold in birchbark baskets distinctive to the region in which they were made. Oldsters told their children that on Easter morning the sun would dance. Rising very early to observe this phenomenon was a time-hallowed custom.

It's well if Easter comes early, thus allowing a month or so until the wildest holiday of all: Vappu.

Vappu comes on the eve of May Day, and there is no way to describe it. Anything goes, provided it isn't actually indecent or criminal. Young people find that it is an ideal time to let off steam, and the white caps worn by university students are much in evidence. (Be warned: that graybeard so rakishly white-capped may not be a student just now; has-been students sport theirs, too.) In Helsinki, the long-suffering statue of Havis Amanda is their traditional victim. Droves of students wade across the moat that surrounds her in order to climb up into her stony arms and crown her with their caps. All day long there are parades of students and workers, and by night there's singing, impromptu dancing in the streets, and all manner of revelry. Nobody goes to bed. We would put it down to spring fever—the giddy excitement that comes with the first flush of warm days— and that could certainly account for the high spirits.

Then comes Midsummer, or Juhannus Day, which celebrates the longest day of the year and the feast of Saint John. It's another marathon festival, and the practical Finns celebrate it on a weekend, regardless of the actual day which is longest. The Saturday closest to June 24 is almost like a medieval holiday. All who are able to go to their favorite lake shore, where they build a huge bonfire to be fired at midnight, and dance, and dance, and dance. Although they don't sing "We won't go home until morning," all the same that's what it's about.

Since it was grafted onto a pagan celebration, a number

of superstitions cling to the observance of Midsummer. You must be sure to have birch in the house to insure future happiness. You should also hang a birch wreath on your cow's horns to protect it, and woe betide the cow whose wreath falls off. When the animal brings it home in the evening, it becomes part of her meal for a special invigorating effect. A custom not much practiced now is that of the young girls bathing naked in the meadows of the young men who take their fancy. (It seems likely that the men stayed up to see who their fans were.)

After Juhannus, activities center on more formal festivals. There are ten regular festivals for sure, and perhaps many more. Something for everybody, whatever your taste. Savonlinna has an opera festival. Kaustinen has a four-day gathering of folk-music enthusiasts and performers, and Pori has a festival of jazz. Turku has a music festival of its own, and so does Kuopio. Helsinki tops it all with three "summer weeks" of concerts, outings, and other events. In Tampere the Pyynikki Open Air Theatre, which has a revolving auditorium, treats visitors to drama out of doors. Jyväskylä has an arts festival and public games during the summer.

Pradzniks, Orthodox church ceremonials, are celebrated in the eastern part of Finland. The great wilderness community of Ilomantsi holds as many as three in a year, against the background of old *tsasounas*. These are wooden churches of such timeless beauty that some of them, the Hattuvaara tsasouna in particular, are outstanding among wooden buildings throughout Europe. The traditional festival may honor Petru, or Ilja, or the Virgin Mary. The colorful ceremony, with its costumed procession, incense-filled church, and sonorous ritual is an experience for anyone, regardless of belief.

Finns flock to the exuberant loggers' competitions,

entirely different in mood from the solemn pradzniks. A logger's work demands that he be tough and agile, and the contests to see who among them is bravest and best are filled with excitement. Every competitor shoots dangerous falls balanced on a log. Running on booms, log-rolling, and dancing are all part of these uproarious, thrill-packed celebrations.

The Festival of the Island Harvest celebrates the return of the fishermen, bringing their prime catches to Helsinki. It is a waterfront spectacle at the harbor which is crammed with boats. This is a special thanksgiving; but Finns also celebrate a Thanksgiving day similar to ours.

This is all good practice for the Big Month, December.

It starts out nicely with Advent, known to the Finns as Pikkujoulu ("Little Christmas"). It's not so little: the pre-Christmas excitement starts building up with parties, much as it does for us.

The Finns take time out from festivities December 6 for a solemn, symbolic observance. It's Independence Day, but it is in no way like our exuberant Fourth of July.

Imagine yourself, in the dark, cold predawn hours, standing quietly in the snow with thousands of shivering spectators. Waiting. At last you see, coming down the broad street, a parade of torches held aloft by silent students. A wall of flags on tall staves follows. There is one flag—a blue cross on white—for each year of Finland's independence. At Mannerheim's grave the marchers find places, and the air is shattered by a burst of song as the Finnish national anthem rises from the thousands of young throats.

And that's it. You go home. No firecrackers, no beer busts. Instead, a solemn recognition of the price it cost to keep Finland free. Elsewhere in the cemeteries, flickering candles show that those who gave their lives in Finland's defense are not forgotten.

From the Swedes has been borrowed the Lucia Day celebration, December 13. It begins at the crack of dawn when a young girl of the family acts as Lucia, the bringer of light. She rises before the rest of the house, dresses in a white robe, and crowns herself with a wreath of lighted candles. Then she wakens the others by serving them Saint Lucia buns and coffee in bed. She herself is feted at the hearty breakfast that follows. The observance is probably a legacy of pagan days when the approaching darkness of the shortest days of the year, which in the far north were completely dark, brought a need for reassurance. Lucia means "light." The Lucia whose fame is celebrated was a young Christian martyr from Sicily.

Along comes Christmas Eve, and here the fun begins. Traditional activities are carried out in the home. There's the dinner, a special one that includes lipeä kala. This is horrible-smelling codfish, but if you can once get close enough to eat it, you become addicted. There is also a Christmas ham and a special rice pudding in which, somewhere, there is *one* almond. The person who gets it is lucky in more ways than one. Not only does or she get a special treat, but the year ahead will be filled with good fortune. (At one time it meant that if the recipient was a young girl, she would be married within the year, but this may not be considered all that lucky anymore.)

Christmas Eve is the time when the gifts are given out—and who does that? The Christmas goat, that's who. Yes, the Christmas goat. He is the descendant of an ancient pagan symbol, who somehow got promoted from the personification of the Devil's emissary to a jovial, boisterous figure in a shaggy fur coat who makes his appearance on a bicycle. His name is Joulupukki (Joulu is the word for Christmas, pronounced "Yule-oo"). Sometimes he appears as the familiar, white-bearded Santa Claus, who may arrive in a sled drawn by real, rather than airborne, reindeer. In either case, he goes through the rigamarole of asking if the children have been good and hands out the presents their parents have thoughtfully provided in secret.

And this brings us to an important question. Is Santa Claus, our own Christmas elf, a Finn? Of course he is. It seems incredible that we haven't realized it before. Where else would you find a man with plenty of reindeer? Where but in northern Finland are there long dark evenings for making toys and shy and gentle beings to help? And the jolly, teasing personality just fits a Finn. "Santa" even sounds like a Finn name, though to be truthful, Saint Nicholas wasn't much revered in Finland of old. Now that we know, we'll have a better idea of where to address our letters in the begging season.

There is one holiday in which Americans are interested that is observed only in Kuopio, for the simple reason that it is not a true Finnish holiday at all. Most Finns haven't heard of it, but Kuopio, being a sister city to Minneapolis, has been informed and can no longer be excused for ignoring it.

It started as a joke, when certain fun-loving members of a department store staff in Virginia, Minnesota, decided to turn the tables on their Finnish manager. On Saint Patrick's Day he had been guilty of the heinous heresy of refusing to be impressed by the Irish claims for their saint. Pooh, said he, Finns have an even greater hero named Urho, and he told tall tales of the saint's mighty prowess. His staff bided their time. On the day which he had named as the feast day of Saint Urho, they greeted him with a hand-carved nutcracker purporting to be the image of the saint, a frog, and a hand-lettered scroll on which an Irish lass (no less) had written a pidgin-Finn rhyme that sang the deeds of his legendary hero.

It was meant only as a bit of mild teasing to be shared among themselves. But a reporter was present, and the next day the hoax hit the front page of the *Mesabi Daily News*. Finns of the area, needing a midwinter frolic during cabin fever season, seized upon it with glee. In the space of only a few years (the original rhyme was written in 1956), the idea spread until the celebration is now observed in several states, with governors proclaiming with straight faces the significance of Saint Urho's Tay (*not* "Day").

His name was not a random choice. He was the namesake of the doughty president of Finland, Urho Kekkonen. Originally the story went that Saint Urho, a strong, brave Finn, saved his country from an influx of frogs by the simple expedient of asking them to leave, and for this deed was to be revered forever. The first date settled upon for this occasion was May 24, but later wags set the date as March 16, thus superseding by one day the Irish festival of Saint Patrick. The enemy he drove from Finland underwent a metamorphosis from frog to grasshopper, and this now seems to be the accepted version. The elaborate fabrication that now goes with the holiday was published in the *Daily Journal* of International Falls, Minnesota:

One of the lesser known, but extraordinary legends of ages past is the legend of St. Urho, patron saint of the Finnish vineyard workers.

Before the last glacial period, the legend goes, wild grapes grew with abundance in the area now known as Findland [sic]. Archeologists have uncovered evidence of this fact scratched on the thigh bones of giant bears that once roamed northern Europe.

The grapes were threatened by a plague of grasshoppers until Urho banished the lot of them with "Heinasirkka, heinasirkka, mene taalta hiiteen." In memory of this impressive demonstration of the power of the Finnish language, at sunrise each March 16, Finnish women and children dressed in royal purple and nile green gather around the shores of the many lakes in Finland and chant what St. Urho chanted many, many years ago:

"Heinasirkka, heinasirkka, mene taalta hiiteen."
Which translated means:

"Grasshopper, grasshopper, go away."
The adult males dressed in green costumes gather on the hills overlooking the lakes, listen to the chant, then kicking out like grasshoppers, slowly disappear to change costumes from green to purple. The celebration ends with singing and dancing polkas and schottisches and drinking grape juice, though these activities may occur in varying sequences.

Colors for the day are royal purple and nile green.

No one takes it seriously, but everyone pretends to. Here is the "poem" that started it all, updated with grasshoppers as the villains instead of frogs and the corrected date.

Ode to Saint Urho

Ooksie, kooksie, koolama, vee!
Santa Urho is ta poy for me.
He sase out ta hopperce as pik as pirts.
Nefer pefore haf I heart tose vorts.
He really tolt tose puks off kreen—
Prafest Finn I efer seen.
Some celeprate for Saint Pat unt hiss nakes,
Put Urho poika cot fhat it takes.
He cot tall unt trong from feelia sour
Unt ate kalla moyakka efery hour.
Tat's fhy tat kuy could sase tose peetles
Fhat crew as tick as chack bine neetles.
So let's gif a cheer in our pest vay
On ta sixteent of Marts, Saint Urho's Tay!

If you are defeated by the Finnglish, it may be translated as follows:

> One, two, three, five!
> Saint Urho is the boy for me.
> He chase[d] out the hoppers as big as birds.
> Never before have I heard those words.
> He really told those bugs of green—
> Bravest Finn I ever seen.
> Some celebrate for Saint Pat and his snakes,
> But Urho-boy got what it takes.
> He got tall and strong from *viili* sour,
> And ate *kalla mojakka* [fish soup] every hour.
> That's why that guy could chase those beetles
> That grew as thick as jackpine needles.
> So let's give a cheer in our best way
> On the sixteenth of March, Saint Urho's Tay!

There's another holiday for each Finn that he may celebrate in his own style. On the Finnish calendar, every day has a saint's name. February 3 is Hugo, February 16 is Julia, June 24 is John (Juhannus, as you may recall), and so on. But you need not receive at birth the name of the saint on whose day you were born. Instead, receiving the name of your parents' choice, you will find that your real birthday is ignored, and your name day celebrated instead. This makes it easier, and your spouse has no excuse for forgetting it because it is on the calendar. All with the same name celebrate together. For instance, if your name is Nyyrikki, you and everyone else with that name will celebrate on January 9. Those named Vappu have their big day on May 1. The day for Urho is June 17, which is sadly out of step with the mock holiday that Finnish Americans have been promoting, and shows a shocking lack of concern for tradition.

A voileipäpöytä ("bread and butter table") is a Finnish feast in the Scandinavian tradition.

CHAPTER 18

GOOD TASTE

HERE'S AN AXIOM to guide you in your experiments with Finnish cuisine: The favorite Finn food is "fin" food.

This love affair with fish came about quite naturally. After all, it is the easiest and most abundant food to be had. This doesn't mean that the Finns regard it as too "everyday" to be truly festive or ever grow tired of it. On the contrary, they have devised so many ways to prepare it that it's inescapable. If you stay anywhere for more than half an hour, you're apt to be offered fish.

Not that their diet is restricted to seafood. More than forty pounds of beef per person are consumed annually and as much pork. Finns are fond of sausage, especially reindeer, and they're adventurous eaters. Your true Finn will not quail at the thought of anything anyone from any tradition wants to serve as food.

Finns have three stout meals a day. There is breakfast (*sami aamiainen*), lunch (*lounas*), and dinner (*paivallinen*), which is usually served about 7 P.M. This gives you plenty of time for a leisurely evening of conversation and sauna. In between there may be any number of snacks, and the coffee pot is ready to go at any time.

Such is the hospitality of Finland that any diet a visitor may hope to follow is doomed. Your worst enemy is the *voileipäpöytä*, a Finnish version of what the Swedes call a *smörgåsbord*. Fearsome though it sounds, the danger lies in its insidious attraction. The name means "bread and butter table," but it's a far cry from the lowly sandwich. It is a beautiful display of snack foods arranged with eye appeal to tempt the most determined dieter. Fish always appears in one or more forms along with cold meats, cheeses, hard-boiled eggs, pickles, artfully cut vegetables and, of course, a variety of breads. Whether you're a gourmet, gourmand, or just a good trencherman, the voileipäpöytä will make your mouth water.

The food of Finland tends to be wholesome, natural, and honest. There's no attempt to disguise poor quality meat with delectable sauces, and although Finns like the flavor of dill with fish, cinnamon and ginger with sweets, cardamom in sweet breads, and allspice in meat, they have no great preoccupation with herbs and spices. About the greatest concession they make to outside tastes is coffee, and there they have capitulated utterly. With less than one-twelfth the population of Great Britain, they use nine times as much coffee!

The Finns also drink great quantities of milk, and it's worth noting that they make the best hot chocolate in Scandinavia. Visitors who have a yen for stronger stuff should try two rare and delicious liqueurs: Mesimarja, made from arctic bramble berries, and Lakka, from the delicate cloud-berries. Vodka is, of course, available (there's an excellent brand called Finlandia that is exported to the United States) as well as Akvavit, gin, brandy, and potato wine. Remember, the Finns raise potatoes, rye, barley, and other grains, so there's raw material available to use in the ancient recipes.

One delicacy the Finns are famous for is *viili*, a yogurtlike milk dish, which comes in two styles: long and short. Long viili, the kind old Finns insist is the only one, can be stretched in long strings when lifted on a spoon. It can be made only if you have a real Finn viili culture to start it, and the purists insist that even then it must be made from whole raw milk. If the starter is available, all that's involved is stirring it into milk that is at room temperature and allowing the mixture to stand overnight. The next morning it is coagulated and ready to be refrigerated for later consumption, if you have the courage.

It's only fitting to introduce the sampler of Finnish recipes that follows with instructions for short viili. All of the recipes are typically Finnish even though they call for ingredients which, for the most part, are easily found in American supermarkets.

Short *Viili*

Short viili is a simple matter. You may make an approximation of it that will pass with the best, using buttermilk as a starter. No mysterious rites are involved.

1   to 2 tablespoons cultured buttermilk
½   cup milk

Let milk warm to room temperature and combine with buttermilk in a custard cup. Place in a slightly warm spot (on the pilot light of a gas stove is a good place, if it's not too warm), cover loosely to keep the dust out, and leave it overnight. Don't shake it, or it may become watery. In the morning the viili should have the texture of gelatin. If not, let it stand until it does coagulate. Chill in the refrigerator, and when you're ready for a taste treat, season with salt and eat with dark bread or sprinkle with sugar and cinnamon. *Serves 1.*

Juusto

(Squeaky Cheese)

This baked cheese used to be served after funerals. Because of its texture, it squeaks as you chew it.

1   quart skim milk
1   rennet tablet
1   tablespoon water

Preheat oven to 500°. Heat milk to lukewarm (110°) and remove from heat. Dissolve rennet in water and stir into milk. The milk will coagulate. Pour into a colander lined with cheesecloth and let it drain. When fairly dry, place in baking pan and flatten to about a 6-inch circle. Bake at 500° for 10 minutes. Drain off any juice that has accumulated during baking and salt lightly. Serve chilled or fried in butter.
Serves 6 to 8.

Kalakeitto

(Fish Soup)

Fish soup (*kala mojakka* in Finnglish) is something that Finland is always accused of, though if you look into the matter, you'll find that every nation makes it. Non-Finns love to tell horror stories of fish heads floating in the kalakeitto, but that's just so much slander. Here are two versions. If you're not sure you'll like fish soup, start off with style I and work up to style II gradually.

I. *Kalakeitto* That Everybody Likes

3   strips bacon
2   tablespoons onion, chopped

¼ cup celery, chopped
1 8-ounce can mixed vegetables
1 cup evaporated milk
1 8-ounce can salmon *or* ½ pound salmon fillets

Fry bacon until crisp. Drain, crumble, and set aside. Sauté onion and celery in remaining bacon fat until tender. Drain excess fat. Drain canned salmon and flake, removing skin and bones. Add salmon, vegetables with their liquid, and milk. Heat to serving temperature. Ladle into bowls and sprinkle bacon bits on top. If using fillets, cut up in small pieces and simmer until tender, about 10 to 15 minutes. *Serves 2.*

II. *Kalakeitto* the Old Country Way

If you like New England clam chowder, you'll find that this soup takes the chill off a wintery day with Finnish flair.

2 to 3 medium potatoes, peeled and quartered
1 medium onion, quartered
1 cup water
1 teaspoon salt
3 whole allspice (optional)
3 whole peppercorns
½ pound fish fillets (whitefish, trout, or pike)
1 tablespoon flour
1 tablespoon butter, melted
¼ cup milk
1 cup evaporated milk
 Dill, chopped
 Parsley, chopped

Place potatoes and onion in kettle and add seasonings. Add 1 cup water or enough to cover. Bring to a boil and cook until tender, about 10 minutes. Reduce heat to simmer and lay fish, in fillets or cut up, on top of vegetables. Cover and simmer gently until fish flakes easily, about 10 minutes. Meanwhile, stir flour into melted butter, stirring until smooth. Add the ¼ cup milk and stir the mixture gently into the soup. Add the evaporated milk and heat until slightly thickened. Ladle into bowls and sprinkle with fresh dill and parsley.

Serves 2.

Graavilohi

(Salted Salmon)

Other immigrants to the United States sometimes referred to Finns as "raw fish eaters," because they cured fish by this method. No cooking is needed, and it's ready to eat in 24 hours.

2   tablespoons salt
2   teaspoons sugar
1   or 2 salmon fillets (about 1 pound total)
2   tablespoons dried dillweed

Combine salt and sugar and rub lightly into fillets. Spread remaining salt-sugar mixture in the bottom of a glass dish, lay fillets on top, and sprinkle with dillweed. Cover and refrigerate for 24 hours. To serve, slice thinly on the diagonal and form into curls.

If you're in a hurry and don't mind a stronger taste, you can cure the fish by placing it in a brine of 1 quart water and 4 tablespoons salt (with some dillweed, of course). Chill in the refrigerator for about 6 hours. The Finns themselves once used seawater, but even if you have seawater handy, you probably don't care to use it on food.

Tomaatisilakat

(Smelts in Tomato Sauce)

If you live in an area where there's a mad dash to the streams during the spring smelt run and successful dashers unload their catch on the whole neighborhood, you might like to serve the tiny fish in the Finnish manner.

1 pound smelts, cleaned and with heads and tails removed
1 2-ounce can anchovy fillets
1/3 cup tomato paste
½ cup evaporated milk
2 tablespoons butter

Preheat oven to 400°. The smaller the smelts, the better. Remove backbone and insert a strip of anchovy in each. Place in a greased baking dish. Combine tomato and milk and spread over fish. Dot with butter. Bake at 400° for 20 minutes, until browned and slightly crusty.
Serves 3 to 4.

Kalakukko

Kukko means "rooster," so this dish translates into English as "fish rooster." Don't ask me why. It's really a fish pie, or pasty, baked in a rye crust.

2 cups rye flour
½ cup white flour
1 teaspoon salt
½ to 2/3 cup water
1 tablespoon oil
1 pound small fish (smelt, perch, or trout), cleaned and with heads and tails removed
6 strips bacon

Preheat oven to 400°. Combine flours and salt. Stir in oil and just enough water to make a stiff dough. Form into a ball and, on a lightly floured surface, roll out in a circle 1 inch thick. Sprinkle with flour. Alternate layers of fish and bacon strips in middle of circle. Fold edges of dough up over filling so that pasty has a football shape. Brush edges with water to seal and keep juices in. Bake at 400° for 1 hour.

Remove from oven and lower temperature to 300°. Wrap pasty in aluminum foil and bake for 3 hours. Remove from oven and wrap foil package in newspapers and cover with more foil. Turn off oven and bake for 2 to 3 hours longer in slowly cooling oven to soften the crust. Then it's ready to eat, and believe it or not, the bones will be edible. Sliced cold, kalakukku makes a good snack.
Serves 4 to 6.

Ravut
(Crayfish)

When crayfish are in season—from mid-July to mid-September—Finns sport shiny chins glossed by the butter in which these delicacies are dipped. The freshwater crayfish looks like a miniature lobster and, like its larger seagoing cousin, is cooked alive by being plunged into boiling water.

Allow 12 crayfish per serving. Put enough water in a large kettle to cover generously. Add 2 tablespoons salt, 1 teaspoon sugar, and 1 teaspoon dill per quart of water. Bring to a boil and add the crayfish, 10 or so at a time, letting the water come to a boil again after each addition. Cook, covered, for about 5 to 7 minutes, or until the crayfish turn red and their tails curl down. Cook only until a crack shows between the tail and body. Chill crayfish in the water in which they were cooked. Serve with melted butter.

Lasimestarinsilli

(Pickled Herring)

The Baltic herring is Finland's gift from the sea. If you like to buy it in jars, try making your own from this old recipe.

1½ to 2 cups tarragon vinegar
½ cup sugar
2 teaspoons whole allspice
3 whole bay leaves
1 teaspoon whole cloves
½ to ¾ pound salt herring
2 medium onions, sliced
2 to 4 carrot curls
2 teaspoons mustard seed
2 teaspoons horseradish

Combine the vinegar, sugar, and spices and heat to boiling. Let cool. Cut up herring into 1-inch pieces, leaving the skin on. In 2 wide-mouthed pint jars, alternate herring with slices of onion. To make carrot curls, pare carrot and then peel off very thin lengthwise slices. In each jar place 1 or 2 carrot curls for color, 1 teaspoon mustard seed, and 1 teaspoon horseradish. Pour pickling solution over herring, cover tightly, and refrigerate for 1 or 2 days before serving. Keeps for about 2 weeks in the refrigerator.
Makes 2 pints.

Lipeä Kala

(Lye-soaked Codfish)

Only the very stouthearted or those indoctrinated in their youth approach this dish without suspicion. Once converted, they fall upon lipeä kala with cries of glee when it makes its appearance in December, while those unlucky enough to be seated beside them at the table sit with averted heads and handkerchiefs to noses. Everyone should try it at least once.

In times past the cook had to soak the fish in lye water for several days, and then rinse it in fresh water for several days more. She had to start three weeks before Christmas if she wanted it for the family dinner. Nowadays you can buy it already processed, even in American supermarkets, where it may go by the name of *lutfisk* (Swedish) or *lutefisk* (Norwegian).

To cook, merely simmer in a stainless steel or enameled stockpot (it turns aluminum black) in a couple of quarts of water until it is translucent and tender but not falling apart. Lift it onto a platter and serve with melted butter or cream sauce.

To bake, place in a greased baking dish, sprinkle with salt and cover with foil. Bake at 350° for 30 to 40 minutes.

Come on, give it a try. After all, that's what made the Finns brave!

Joulukinkku

(Christmas Ham)

Celebrating Christmas in style used to mean putting the Christmas ham to soak in salt water two weeks ahead of time, after which it was smoked in the savu sauna and at last baked in a crust. You can prepare a reasonable facsimile.

1	large ham (9 or 10 pounds)
7	cups rye flour
3	cups water (or less)
1	cup water

Preheat oven to 325°. Place ham in heavy roasting pan, on rack if possible. Mix flour with enough water to make a stiff dough. Flatten with wet hands and mold over top and sides of ham. Pour 1 cup water into roasting pan.

Bake, uncovered, for ½ hour per pound. (Allow 5 or 6 hours for complete baking time.) If pan becomes dry, add more water as necessary. If crust begins to become over-brown, cover with foil to prevent burning.

When done, allow ham to rest 10 minutes before slicing. Remove crust to serve separately, to be dipped in pan juices. Serve with hot sweet mustard such as Chinese mustard. *Serves 18 to 20.*

Lihapyöryköitä
(Meat Balls)

Finns like meat, and they like to know what it tastes like, so they avoid smothering it in sauces. They prepare beef, pork, lamb, reindeer, and elk in roasts, stews, and the like. Ground meat shows up in meat pasties or tarts, and these character-istic meatballs with the ever present allspice.

½	cup bread crumbs
½	cup evaporated milk
1	pound ground beef
1	medium onion, chopped
1	egg
2	teaspoons salt
½	teaspoon allspice
2	tablespoons butter
2	tablespoons flour
1½	cups evaporated milk

Soak bread crumbs in the ½ cup evaporated milk and combine with the ground beef, onion, egg, and seasonings. Form into 1-inch balls and brown in melted butter. Remove from pan. Add flour to drippings in pan and stir until smooth. Blend in the 1½ cups evaporated milk and cook, over medium heat, stirring constantly, until slightly thickened. Add water if gravy becomes too thick. Return meatballs to pan, cover, and simmer 30 minutes, or bake in a 350° oven for 30 minutes.
Serves 3 to 4.

Piirakkaa

(Pasty)

The Cornish are often given credit for the pasties which were such an important part of the miner's lunch, but the Finns have a version of their own with a rye piecrust. Originally, the filling was a rice or potato mixture, but sometime in their history the Finns began turning out cheese and meat-and-vegetable piirakkaa, which might be baked or fried in butter. Made in miniature, they show up today as appetizers, but the traditional piirakkaa was the size of half a pie.

1	cup lard
1½	cups rye flour
1½	cups all-purpose flour
1	teaspoon salt
½	to 2/3 cup water
1	cup minced round steak (not ground!)
½	cup potato, finely cubed
1/3	cup carrot, finely cubed
¼	cup onion, chopped
¼	cup rutabaga, chopped (optional)

¼ cup beef gravy or other liquid
1 tablespoon butter

Preheat oven to 350°. Combine flours and salt and cut in lard with pastry blender until mixture is like meal. Stir in water, a little at a time, until a stiff dough forms. Shape into 6 small balls. On a lightly floured surface, roll out into 7-inch circles.

For filling, combine steak, vegetables, and gravy. Spread on half of each circle to within ½ inch of the edge. Dot with butter. Brush edge of other half with water, fold over, and seal. Cut slit in top to allow steam to escape. Bake at 350° for 30 minutes or until puffed and bubbly and vegetables are tender when pricked with a fork through the steam vent. *Serves 6.*

Rieska

(Flat Bread)

Pictures of Finland long ago show disks of flat bread curing on the rafters, a year's supply at a time.

1 package active dry yeast
2 cups warm water (110°)
1 teaspoon salt
4½ to 5 cups rye *or* whole wheat flour

Dissolve yeast in warm water. Combine salt and 2 cups of the flour and stir in dissolved yeast. Add enough of the remaining flour to make a stiff dough. Turn out on a lightly floured surface and knead until smooth and elastic, about 10 minutes. Place in a greased mixing bowl, cover, and let rise until doubled in size.

Preheat oven to 450°. Turn out on a lightly floured sur-

face and divide into four portions, shaping each into a round
ball. On a greased cookie sheet, roll out to ¼ inch thickness.
Using the customary tomato can or a biscuit cutter, cut a
hole in the center and prick entire surface with a fork. Let
stand for 15 minutes; then bake at 450° for 15 minutes.
Rieska will be firm yet rubbery. Allow to dry uncovered
overnight.
Makes 4 round, flat loaves.

Hapenleipä
(Sour Rye Bread)

If you really want to be authentic about this, you have to
start the starter two days ahead and have a cozy kitchen. If
you are a purist, you can make starter without yeast by
letting it ferment four days and adding the yeast just before
you stir in the additional flour for the bread dough.

Sourdough Starter

1   tablespoon active dry yeast
2   cups warm water *or* beer *or* buttermilk (110°)
2   cups rye flour
1   teaspoon salt
2   cups *each* rye and all-purpose flour

Dissolve yeast in warm liquid and stir in 1 cup of the rye
flour. Let stand in a warm place (80 to 90°) for 1 day. Add
the salt and 1 more cup rye flour and let it stand for another
day. It will give off a fragrance not unlike a brewery's. On the
third day add 2 cups each rye and all-purpose flour or
enough to make a stiff dough. Knead, let rise, shape, and
bake as directed under Shortcut Sourdough.
Makes 2 loaves.

Shortcut Sourdough

2   packages active dry yeast
2   cups warm water *or* beer *or* buttermilk (110°)
3   cups rye flour
3   cups all-purpose flour

Dissolve yeast in warm liquid and stir in 2 cups of the rye flour. Let stand in a warm place (80 to 90°) overnight. Next morning, stir in 1 cup rye flour and 3 cups all-purpose flour, or enough to make a stiff dough. Turn out on a lightly floured surface and knead until smooth and elastic, about 10 minutes. Place in a greased bowl, cover, and let rise until doubled, about 1 to 2 hours.

Divide in half and shape into 2 balls. On a lightly floured surface, roll each into a circle about 12 inches across. Place on a greased baking sheet and cut a hole in the center with a biscuit cutter or tomato can. (If you'd rather, shape dough into 2 long loaves like French bread by rolling each out into an oblong and rolling up, starting with the long side. Tuck ends under and slash tops with a sharp knife.) Cover and let rise until doubled in size. Preheat oven to 375°.

Prick round loaves all over with fork. Bake at 375° for 30 minutes. Brush with melted butter and cover with towel while cooling to soften crust.
Makes 2 loaves.

Pulla

(Sweet Bread)

This cardamom-flavored sweet bread is sometimes used for Saint Lucia buns, the special goodies served for breakfast on Saint Lucia's Day.

1   cup milk, scalded
½   cup butter
2   eggs
½   cup sugar
½   teaspoon salt
1   package active dry yeast
1   teaspoon ground cardamom
4   to 5 cups all-purpose flour
1   egg
½   cup sugar
     Slivered almonds (optional)

Scald milk and combine with butter, 2 eggs, ½ cup sugar, and salt. Cool to lukewarm. Stir in yeast, cardamom, and enough flour to make a stiff dough. (If you prefer a more tender dough and don't mind extra puttering, mix together the scalded milk, sugar, salt, yeast, and cardamom. Blend in the eggs and stir until well beaten. Mix in 2 cups of flour and work the butter in thoroughly. Add the remaining flour.)

Turn out on a lightly floured surface and knead until smooth and elastic, about 10 minutes. Divide into three equal portions. Shape each portion into a long whip and braid the three strips together, pinching at the ends to prevent unraveling. Lay on a greased baking sheet, cover, and let rise until doubled in size, about 1½ hours.

Preheat oven to 400°. Make glaze by beating remaining egg with ½ cup sugar and brush loaf. Sprinkle with slivered almonds if desired. Bake at 400° for 20 to 30 minutes, or until golden.

For Saint Lucia buns, roll out the dough to ½-inch thickness and cut it into 5 x 1-inch strips. Using 2 strips for each bun, lay one on the other at right angles and fold the four tips into the center. Put one raisin at the folded tip of each strip. Let rise until double, brush with egg glaze, and bake at 375° for 15 minutes.

Sekahedelmäkeitto

(Fruit Soup)

Fruit soup is a traditional Scandinavian dessert at Christmas. Feel free to brew it to your taste with your own assortment of prunes, raisins, and dried apricots, apples, and pears.

1	1½-pound package mixed dried fruits
1	cinnamon stick
1	cup sugar *or* honey
3	quarts water
2	tablespoons cornstarch
¼	cup cold water

Simmer fruits, cinnamon, and sugar or honey for 1 hour in water. Blend cornstarch with the cold water and add to the soup, stirring until slightly thickened. If you wish, you may substitute 2 tablespoons quick-cooking tapioca for the cornstarch-water mixture.
Serves 10 to 12.

Riispuuro

(Rice Pudding)

Riispuuro is a traditional conclusion to the Christmas feast. Hiding an almond in the pudding adds an excitement that belies its bland taste since the finder can look forward to good luck in the coming year.

1½	cups water
½	teaspoon salt
1	cup rice
2	cups milk

1   almond
     Cinnamon-sugar
     Light cream

Heat water to boiling and stir in salt and rice. Simmer 20 minutes. Add milk, cover loosely, and set over very low heat until milk has been absorbed. Put in the almond. Serve warm and pass cinnamon-sugar and light cream. May also be served cold with fruit soup.
Serves 6.

Ruusunmarjakeitto

(Rose Hip Soup)

The wild fruits of Finland—blueberries, strawberries, and lingonberries—are featured in many desserts. Here is a recipe for the "fruits" of the wild rose—the red, fleshy seed pods that are called hips. Did you know that three rose hips have as much vitamin C as one orange?

2   cups dried rose hips
1   quart water
1/3 to ½ cup sugar
2   tablespoons cornstarch
¼   cup cold water
     Whipped cream
     Slivered almonds

If you have fresh rose hips, use about 2½ cups. Wash them well and remove blossom ends. Soak dried rose hips overnight in water to soften. Add enough water to equal 1 quart and simmer, covered, until tender, 30 to 45 minutes. Strain through cheesecloth over a colander to remove seeds. Add sugar to taste. Return soup to saucepan. Blend cornstarch

with the ¼ cup cold water and add to the soup, stirring until slightly thickened. Chill before serving and garnish with whipped cream and slivered almonds.
Serves 4.

Mämmi
(Rye Pudding)

A traditional Easter dessert. For the real thing you ought to have rye malt for sweetening and a birch basket to bake it in.

2   cups water
¼   cup dark molasses
    Dash salt
2   tablespoons rye flour
½   cup rye flour
1   tablespoon grated orange peel
2   tablespoons raisins
    Sugar
    Light cream

Combine water, molasses, salt, and the 2 tablespoons rye flour. Bring to a boil, beating constantly with a wire whisk. Cover and let stand for 1 hour. Preheat oven to 275°.

Stir in the remaining flour, orange peel, and raisins. Pour into greased 1-quart casserole and bake, uncovered, at 275° for 3 hours. Cover and chill. Sprinkle with sugar and pass sugar and light cream.
Serves 4.

Kaleivät

(Cookies)

If you are looking for a typically Finnish cookie, you might consider Runebergintorttut (Runeberg tarts), which are little pielets made with a cookie dough pastry, filled with almonds and a dab of currant jelly, and topped with a powdered sugar frosting. Another Finnish specialty is Alexanterintortut, (Czar Alexander's tarts), a sugar cookie sandwich filled with jam and frosted. Gingersnaps (*pepparkakor* or *piparkakut*) can be made according to any standard recipe but use plenty of spice. For a recipe calling for 3 cups of flour, use 1 *tablespoon* each of ginger and cinnamon.

Nissu Nassu

(Little Christmas Pigs)

This spicy dough makes a good gingerbread man or other crisp rolled cookie, but in Finland at Christmas the favorite shape is little piggies. (Recipe courtesy of Beatrice Ojakangas)

2/3	cup butter or margarine
¾	cup brown sugar, packed
2½	cups flour
1½	teaspoons baking soda
1½	teaspoons ground cloves
2	teaspoons ground ginger
1	tablespoon ground cinnamon
4	to 6 tablespoons warm water

Preheat oven to 400°. Cream butter and sugar. Sift dry ingredients together and add to sugar-butter mixture. Add water a tablespoonful at a time, until dough forms ball. If too soft, chill before rolling. On a lightly floured surface, roll out to ⅛-inch thickness and cut with a floured cookie cutter. (True nissu nassu are pig shaped.) Bake on a greased and floured cookie sheet for 8 to 10 minutes. Spread with powdered sugar frosting if you like.
Makes about 3 dozen cookies.

Finska Kakor
(Finnish Cake)

Try this rich and tender pastry dough as is or use it for filled cookies.

1	cup butter, softened
1¼	cups cottage cheese *or* cream cheese, softened
2½	cups all-purpose flour
1	egg white, unbeaten
	Almonds or roasted chestnuts, chopped

Preheat oven to 400°. Cream butter and cheese with fork and stir in flour. On a lightly floured surface, roll out to ¼-inch thickness. Brush with egg white and sprinkle with nuts and cut into 1x2½-inch strips. For a filled cookie, omit egg white and nuts. Roll out to ⅛-inch thickness and cut into circles with a biscuit cutter. Place 1 teaspoon sweetened stewed prunes or apricots, chopped and drained, on half the circle. Fold over to form a crescent. Bake on ungreased cookie sheet at 400° for 8 to 10 minutes, whichever variation you choose.
Makes about 3 dozen cookies.

Ruiskakkuja

(Rye Cookies)

½   cup butter or margarine, melted
½   cup sugar
1½ teaspoons baking powder
1   cup rye flour
1   cup all-purpose flour
3   to 4 tablespoons cold water

Combine butter with dry ingredients. Sprinkle with just enough cold water to moisten—no more than 4 tablespoons. Chill. Preheat oven to 350°.

On a lightly floured surface, roll out ⅛-inch thick and cut into desired shapes. Bake at 350° on greased cookie sheets 8 to 10 minutes.

Makes about 3 dozen cookies.

Sima

(Punch)

This will put you into the "spirit" of things for Vappu, a Finnish celebration on May Day Eve.

4   quarts water
1   cup brown sugar *or* honey
1¼ cups granulated sugar
1   teaspoon active dry yeast
2   lemons, peeled and sliced thin
1   tablespoon raisins
    Pinch ginger (optional)
1   cup light beer (optional)

Heat water to boiling and stir in sugars. Cool to lukewarm and add yeast and lemon slices. Let stand overnight in a warm place (80 to 90°).

Place raisins in a 1-gallon jug. Add ginger and beer if desired. Strain yeast mixture through cheesecloth into jug. Cover and let stand at room temperature until raisins come to the top of the jug. Chill, tightly capped, in refrigerator. *Makes 1 gallon.*

Michael Agricola, Bishop of Turku, published the first Finnish alphabet book and followed it up with a translation of the New Testament in 1548.

CHAPTER 19

AN ORPHAN LANGUAGE

ONE REASON that's given for the legendary taciturnity of the Finns is that they have a struggle with their language, too.

It has already been said that Finnish bears no resemblance to any other existing language, even those thought to be related. Think, for a moment, how singular this is.

In the case of other world languages that have a common root, it's possible to manage some basic communication. A Norwegian can understand a Swede, and a Dane can decipher German. Many words and expressions in the Latin languages are almost interchangeable: there's virtually no difference between *senhor, señor,* and *signor.* Even English has a number of foreign words in common use, like garage and diesel, that would make a foreigner feel at home. But nothing has made a dent in the language of the Finns. It was, is, and presumably always will be just that—the language of the Finns.

As for the vaunted relationship between it and the Magyar tongue of Hungary, it takes the eye of a scientist with X-ray vision to see it. A Finn can no more engage in conversation with a Hungarian than an Eskimo with a Hottentot.

Such incomprehensible speech must be impossible to learn, non-Finns decide, with the result that hardly anyone who hasn't a drop of Finnish blood even tries. This is really too bad, for it is not at all the truth. Finnish is a simple, regular language, and it has an advantage over Greek and

Russian, for example, in that it uses the Roman alphabet that is familiar to us.

It's not even as long an alphabet as little American children are expected to master. There is no *b, c, d, q, x, w,* or *z* except in foreign words. So, you see, all those words that seem to go on and on are conjured up out of a nineteen-letter base. Moreover, some letters are decided favorites. Half the dictionary is made up of words beginning with *k, t, p, r,* and *v.*

To make things easier, each consonant has only one pronunciation. *G* shows up only after *n,* giving the sound of ri*ng.* That means you don't need a phonetic key with any word; you say it the way it looks.

The vowels are the same as those you are used to, but they follow Finnish laws. Finns consider English confusing because in our language the same vowel may have two different sounds. Diacritical marks ease the way in Finnish.

a is ah; *ä* is the *a* of r*a*t.

e is always the short *e* of m*e*t.

i sounds something like the first *i* in sp*i*rit, and the way it is pronounced in Spanish is even closer. *ii* is the double *e* in p*ee*k.

o is like *o*h; *ö* is like the *e* in h*e*rb.

u is the *u* of p*u*t; *uu* is *oo.*

y is harder to describe. Try saying it as if you were saying *oo* and *ii* at the same time. It's like the French *u,* if that helps any.

To make things even easier, Finnish is invariably accented on the first syllable.

Simple, isn't it? You are now ready to try a few Finnish words.

    ravinto (food): rah´ veen toe

    lohi (salmon): low´ hee

And names.

    Kekkonen: Kek´ ko nen

    Iittala: Ee´ tah lah (a bit trickier)

To sound genuinely Finnish, you must r-r-roll your *r*'s.

    herra (gentleman): hair´ rrra

Since there is no *d*, *t* does double duty. And *p* takes the place of *b* in all but foreign-derived words. *J* is pronounced like *y* in *y*ou, always. As for *x*, *q*, and *w*, you never meet them. Try a few more.

    kissa (cat): key´ ssssah

    poika (boy): poy´ kah

    tyttö (girl): tiu´ tuh

    hunaja (honey): hoo´ nah yah

    Englanninkieli (English language): Eng´ lan in key´ eh lih

    nainen (woman): nah´ i nen

As you pronounced *nainen*, you noticed something: when you give each written vowel its full value, you come up with diphthongs quite unconsciously. Thus, vowels in combination make up the following diphthongs:

    ai as in *ai*sle

    au as in *ow*l

    ou as in lo*u*ver

    ui as in q*ui*ck

    ei as in n*ei*ghbor

That's it. That's all you need to know. Now you are ready for the ultimate challenge. You can read aloud from the Finnish newspaper. Yes, you can. This is not to say, alas, that you will understand it.

Numbers, once you master the basic ten, can be built upon quite easily. For instance, you count from one to twelve as follows:

1.	*yksi*	7.	*seitsemän*
2.	*kaksi*	8.	*kahdeksan*
3.	*kolme*	9.	*yhdeksän*
4.	*neljä*	10.	*kymmenen*
5.	*viisi*	11.	*yksitoista*
6.	*kuusi*	12.	*kaksitoista*

Fine and dandy. Now, to make the teens, you add-*toista,* just as you did for eleven and twelve.

neljätoista (14)   *viisitoista* (15)

For the added decades, you add *kymmentä* to the number indicating how many tens.

Kaksi-kymmentä (20) is two tens.

Kolme-kymmentä-kaksi (32) is three tens plus two.

Neljä-kymmentä-kahdeksan (48) is four tens plus eight.

And so on, up to *sata,* which is 100.

To further simplify matters, Finnish has no article. "House" is simply house; it is not *a* house or *the* house. Isn't that better than French, where the article has to agree with the noun it accompanies, and there's a different article for one man or several, plus a requirement that single males and females can't use the same article? And in Finnish there's no future tense. No "I will go." Just "I go."

Lest you should think yourself now qualified to speak it,

there are a few pitfalls for the unwary. For instance, the harmless-looking word *kuusi* (spruce), means something quite unacceptable in polite conversation when it is pronounced wrongly.

It must be confessed that this is not the whole story. There is the matter of cases. One writer bewails the fact that there are sixteen cases in Finnish, which is bewildering for Americans who need almost none. He cites, for example, the old town on Finland's eastern coast where a tourist may wish to see a beautiful thirteenth-century stone church with gates of carved wood. If you are content just to name the town, well and good; it is Uusikaupunki. But if you go there, it is Uuleenkaupunkiin: if you talk about it afterwards, you must say Uudestakaupungista. If you live there, matters are even worse: Uudessakaupungissa.

Family names offer an interesting sidelight. Most Finnish surnames have a distinct meaning that describes the family estate in some way. Mäki, which means hill, identifies a number of Finns, some of whom Anglicized their name when they became Americans. Kivi (stone) and Järvi (lake) are other examples. These grow more complicated as they get more specific: Pelto (field) and Niemi (headland) are combined to form Peltoniemi. And there are Kivimäki, Metsamäki, and others, all telling something of the place from which the bearers of these names have come.

The endings *la* or *nen* on surnames correspond to *Mc* and *Mac* in Gaelic, meaning "of" or "from." Thus we have names like Partanen, meaning "son of the bearded one," and Heikkila, meaning "son of Heikki." Mäkinen means "of the hill"; Rajala is "from the border." Finns have also followed the Swedish custom of adding -*son* to the father's name, and frequently a name like Knutson or Gustafson shows direct derivation from the Swedish, identifying its owner as a "Swede-Finn."

Language difficulties should never prevent anyone from visiting Finland. English as a second language is spoken by a majority of Finns, and it is very unlikely that the traveler will find a hamlet so remote that no one can interpret his or her speech. In fact, even if you have a smattering of Finn, it is the safer course. Not even a year ago, a staid traveler, feeling quite confident of her command of Finnish, used her skill to invite a young man to stand beside another elderly woman in her tour group for a photograph. She meant a courteous suggestion, but her choice of words was unfortunate to say the least—what she said was indecent. The young man became hysterical with laughter and could not be persuaded to translate her invitation.

It might be advisable for you to make a survival kit with a packet of 3x5 cards. Print the phrases most likely to succeed on one side of the cards and put their English equivalents on the reverse. Add a pronunciation key if you are brave. A sample card might look like this:

This side to show   This side for
to the Finns: yourself:

| Terve | Hello
(Tehr′ veh) |

Your collection might include the following.

Polite words:

*Good day: *hyvää päivää* (hiu′ v**aa** pie′ v**aa**)

---

*The ä sound, as in r**a**t, is indicated by a boldface **a**.

Good evening: *hyvää ilta* (hiu′ v**aa** eel′ tah)

Good morning: *hyvää huomenta* (hiu′ v**aa** hoo-oh′ men tah)

Please: *miellyttää* (mee′ ell liu t**aa**)

Thank you: *kiitos* (key′ toce)

Excuse me: *anteeksi* (ahnt′ ehk see)

Yes: *kyllä* (kiul′ l**a**)

No: *ei* (ay)

Phrases:

Give me: *Anna minulle* (Ah′ nah moo leh)

How much does it cost? *Kuinka paljo maksaa?* (Kwink′ ah pahl′ yoh maahk′ saah)

What does it say? *Mitä se sanoo?* (Mit′ **a** seh sah′ noh)

What is this? *Mikä tämä on?* (Mee′ k**a** t**a** m**a** ohn)

What time is it? *Paljonko kello on?* (Pahl′ yohn koh kel′ lo ohn)

Where is? *Missä on?* (Mee′ s**a** ohn)

Name words:

coffee: *kahvi* (kah′ vi)

doctor: *tohtori* (toh′ to ree)

food: *ravinto* (rah′ veen toe)

gas (for car): *bensiini* (pent′ see nee)

hotel: *hotelli* (ho′ tel li)

match: *tulitikku* (too′ lee tick oo)

men: *miehet* (mee′ eh het)

milk: *maito* (my' toe)

money: *raha* (rah' hah)

police officer: *poliisi* (poh' lee si)

restroom: *W.C.* (!)

water: *vesi* (veh' si)

women: *nainen* (nah' ee nen)

Place words:

airport: *lentokenttä* (len' toh ken' ta)

bank: *pankki* (pank' key)

garage: *autotalli* (ow' toe tall ee)

hospital: *sairaala* (sigh' raah lah)

railroad station: *rautatieasema* (row' tah tee eh ah' seh mah)

restaurant: *ravintola* (rah' veen toh lah)

store: *kauppa* (cow' pah)

Signs you must read:

Exit: *Ulos*

Go: *Mennä*

No Smoking: *Tupakointi kielletty*

Stop: *Seis*

Wait: *Odottaa*

That's all, except for "I'll be seeing you"—*näkemiin* (na' keh meen).

Of course, you may not need all these words. But if you do, it's a good idea to group them by colors: pink for words of courtesy, green for things you need to ask, and orange for places or things. That way, you won't be fumbling through twenty cards while the train pulls out, when all you need is the one that says "What time is it?"

From the attempt of Finns in America to speak English in the manner of their own mother tongue, a third language has sprung up which, for want of a better word, must be called Finnglish. What it represents is a speech in which an adopted English word has to be used, either because Finnish has no equivalent, or because it names something that was unfamiliar to Finns or hadn't been invented when they emigrated. Most of these borrowed words are Finn-ized by adding the ending *i*. Thus *miner* became *maineri, boss* was *paasi, beer* was *piiri*. An American dessert new to the Finns was *appoli pai*. Actually, one might wonder why some words were borrowed, since Finnish has a perfectly acceptable equivalent. When one hears *haussi* for house, *leeki* for lake, or such words, perhaps it reflects the fact that certain rhythms sound better to the Finnish ear. For the Finn, with his firmly structured language, English is difficult to master. Trying to write in the new language is an even greater challenge, since a bewildering array of sounds may be represented by only one letter and a combination like *ough* can be pronounced in a number of ways. One night-school hopeful once asked plaintively, "Do you spell *quit* wit a wee or a wubble-you?"

Sentence structure is given an obvious Finnglish twist: "Kivit for me tat peeri" translates as "Give me a beer."

Regardless of its idiosyncracies, the Finnish language is worth knowing. It's a key to beautiful poetry and earthy or dramatic literature. It's a means of knowing the minds of these unusual people. In a culture where the greatest magic of primitive wizards was worked with words, what could express more exactly their singular nature than the language that is uniquely their own?

Janice Laulainen, Secretary of the Finnish American Heritage organization in Minneapolis, welcomes Urho Kekkonen, President of Finland, to Minnesota.

CHAPTER 20

THEY CAME IN PEACE

FOR THOSE WHO ARE APT to look upon Finns as Johnny-come-latelys on the American scene, consider this.

Leif Erikson came cruising along these shores in A.D. 1000, and it wouldn't be at all unlikely that good Finn shipwrights built the boat he came on and may even have been along for the ride.

If that's too far-fetched for you, there's the Kensington Runestone. This is a marker which an unsuspecting farmer uncovered near Alexandria, Minnesota, on which is inscribed, in ancient Runic characters, the record of twenty-two Norsemen and eight Swedes (who in those days might well have been a touch Finn) who passed that way in the year 1362. In all fairness it must be conceded that the authenticity of this is hotly disputed, but everyone admits that it could have happened, and it fits very well in Norse history. There's an authenticated account of King Magnus having sent a rescue mission to follow an earlier expedition to America about the right time. Besides, has anyone any better explanation of why the Mandan Indians of North Dakota had blue eyes?

For the real skeptics, there's the 1979 authentication of a Norse coin found on the coast of Maine. Previously misidentified as an English penny, it was actually struck in Norway sometime between 1065 and 1080. That's straight from Kolbjorn Skaare, the world's leading authority on Viking coins. Now if it dropped from the pocket of a Finn . . .

The first Finns who settled in North America made their homes here a mere seven years after the Pilgrims landed, and large numbers of them came to Delaware in the 1630s. These Finns built the first Lutheran church in America.

Finns of Colonial times also deserve credit for introducing the log cabin to the American scene. This style of building, with its evenly hewed logs and dovetailed corners, was so well suited to woodsy wilderness that it took hold rapidly among settlers of other nationalities.

A minority they may have been, but those who saw the Finns admired them. William Penn in 1680 made grateful mention of their contribution to Delaware, and there were notable Finnish settlements in Pennsylvania. One was where Philadelphia is now, and near the city of Chester, there was a village called "Finland."

Take a look at the Declaration of Independence, and you will see that the Finns were right there. The man who cast the deciding vote was none other than John Morton. His Finnish roots went back to a great-grandfather, Martti Martinen, who first saw daylight in 1606, in Rautalampi. Obviously Martti's descendant was in the vanguard of those who Anglicized their names into something more fashionable.

Hold onto your hat for this one—our first president was a Finn!

It's a fact. His name was John Hanson, and he held the office under the Articles of Confederation, some years ahead of the Constitution and the sainted George Washington. The new nation was not yet the "United States" so Hanson lost the honor on a technicality, but he was recognized to the extent of having his picture on a postal card recently.

Finns continued to come in small waves during the 1800s. Only the city of their origin makes it possible for us to identify them, since their passports indicated that they were

Swedish or Russian subjects, but they helped to swell the tide of newcomers to American shores. Sometimes they were sailors who jumped ship and made themselves a new life in seaport cities like Boston, Baltimore, Galveston, and Portland. One crew decided to abandon ship en masse when their vessel was held in New Orleans through fear of British impressment. The discovery of gold in California proved too tempting to many crewmen, who declined to make the return trip they had signed on for. A number of solid Finn citizens braved the rigors of Alaska as long ago as 1840, well before it was in American hands.

Eventually there were Finns in every state, though the greatest numbers were in the states most like Finland. Mining, lumbering, and plenty of rivers and lakes made Michigan, Wisconsin, and Minnesota the preferred spots for settlement in this century. About three-quarters of the immigrating Finns settled there. Others found their way to the copper mines of Butte, Montana, the fisheries of Astoria, Oregon, and the limestone quarries and coal pits of Wyoming. Few Finns settled in cities for long. They took to the land and settled in communities which they enlivened by their co-ops, their love of music and dancing, and their eagerness for education.

When U.S. immigration authorities established quotas, Finland was allowed six hundred per year. This was easily filled. Whatever the reason, it wasn't hard to get Finns to leave home.

A special class of immigrant was young men soon to be inducted into the army of the Russian czar. Understandably, these youths found it hard to get passports but the wily Finns found a way around that. An immigrant already safe in the United States would send his passport home to be used by another man. Some passports made a number of Atlantic crossings, and it must be said that authorities sympathetically overlooked the unusual prevalence of certain recurring names.

Another way of eluding Russian recruiters was practiced by the pastors. These good men, who put humanity before legality, occasionally altered birth certificates to show a man to be older than he actually was. Losing a son to America was preferable to losing him to the Cossacks. Of a quarter-million who left Finland, 90 percent went to America.

So, for one reason or another, the number of American Finns eventually swelled to three hundred thousand. Free from dread of political repercussions and the bitter resentment of a subject minority, they took to their adopted nation with zest. As Franklin D. Roosevelt said, "From the beginning of our history onward, men and women of Finnish blood have played important roles in the development of our country. Their industry, stability, and resourcefulness have made them an important element in American nationality."

Now you will find Finns almost everywhere. Telephone books in mid-American cities have pages of names with recognizably Finnish endings. The retirement communities of Lantana and Fort Worth in Florida are almost completely made up of Finnish Americans. Fitchburg, Massachusetts, has a strong Finnish tradition. In Minnesota there is no county without its Finn. Most, however, are in the northern sector, where the lakes and forests and iron mines are much like home. As Minnesota farmers, they faced the most hopeless of tasks in bringing the thin, stony soil into production. Grace Lee Nute, author of *Rainy River Country,* says that nobody but a Finn would have tried it!

Much of the time immigrants settled in communities where there were already Finns. This happened frequently because one family member who had made the journey would send home a ticket for the one next in line. In any case, it was natural to feel more secure where someone had already paved the way. Finnish immigrants also moved in happily alongside any other Americans. There is even one community of Finns known as French Lake!

It is sometimes hard to track the Finns down after they settled. In their zeal to become Americans, they frequently Anglicized their names. One settler abandoned his ten-letter surname and announced that he would henceforth bear the good American name of Peterson. He then in all innocence gave his children such "American" first names as Vilho, Väinö, Niilo, Osmo, Irja, Kaisa, and Tyynne.

Frequently the Finn had no choice in the matter. A foreman or timekeeper, unable to cope with Kyyhkynen or Saarijarvi, would arbitrarily assign a name such as Mike Brown or Tom Johnson, which the uncomplaining Finn would then carry for the rest of his life. In some cases, realizing that his name could be translated into English, a Finn would use that as his American name. Many people named Maki or Salo became Hill or Woods respectively.

A most important tradition was that of pride in succeeding on their own, using the resources of what Finns call *hartia-pänkki*—a bank whose only collateral is an individual's physical strength and courage. The Finns have a saying: "Strong willpower takes a man even through stone."

Their physical strength is proverbial. Finns were never afraid to settle far from a doctor, and many a Finnish American came into the world with only his or her father in attendance. Accidents required medical care, but for normal illnesses, never. One Finn at the age of eighty-five said that in all his life he had taken only fourteen pills.

Do-it-yourself was something the Finns had always accepted as the natural order of things. They brought it with them to the New World. Some had a better hartia-pänkki than others and accomplished prodigious feats in building farms. One family carried self-sufficiency to such an extent that they maintained the public road near their farm and furnished and operated their own school bus.

Cooperatives proliferated in the Finnish settlements, and Finns formed Finnish American societies like the Knights of Kaleva. Originally formed as help-one-another clubs, they have become treasure-houses of Finnish tradition.

Finns have even established a college, Suomi College, in Hancock, Michigan, where along with more common disciplines the student is imbued with a sense of his Finnish heritage. Archives there and at the University of Minnesota document much of the history of Finnish Americans.

Several organizations in Finland serve to maintain the ties between the Finns at home and those in the United States. The Suomi Society (Suomi-Seura) arranges for visits to the homeland and for Finnish culture seminars in English. It also holds a popular summer festival especially for returning emigrants and their descendants.

The League of Finnish-American Societies has the same goal of Finnish-American friendship. Their special festival is "America Days," and they make an effort to offer grants and fellowships plus warm Finnish hospitality to American students. Finnish students may study in America through ASLA Fulbright scholarships. The American Field Service (AFS) provides opportunities for American high school students to spend a year with a family in Finland and for Finnish students to do likewise in the United States. The American Scandinavian Foundation (ASF) has a similar program with lectures, exhibits, and fellowship exchanges.

A student who wants to spend a year in Finland but hasn't funds of his or her own might do well to apply to the Finnish Ministry of Labor. They have a special program that arranges opportunities for American students to spend a part of the summer in Finland in a Finnish household, where they are received as family members, helping with chores and earning allowances, though their main purpose is to teach English. Some years as many as one hundred young people have been guests of Finland in this program, which began in the early 1950s. More information may be obtained by writing to:

Trainees Exchange Office, Ministry of Labour
Messeniuksenkato 1B/PL 5
Harjoitteljainvaihtotoimisto
00251 Helsinki 25, Finland

FINN FACTS

THE NAME OF THE COUNTRY is Suomi. Suomen Tasavalta means "Finnish Republic." The people are called Suomalainen.

Population: 4,750,000; 59.0% urban
Density: 36.43 per square mile
Language: Finnish 93.5%, Swedish 6.5%
Religion: Lutheran 92%, Russian Orthodox 1.3%
Area: 130,119 square miles (16,173 square miles lost to Russia)
Principal cities: Helsinki, 496,263; Tampere, 166,177; Turku, 164,344
Industries: machinery, metal, shipbuilding, textiles, leather, chemicals, tourism
Monetary unit: markka (4.02 mk. = $1.00)
Per capita income: $5660
Gross National Product: $31.74 billion
Minerals: copper, iron, zinc, lead
Crops: grain, potatoes
Forests: 55% of exports
Government: President — Urho Kekkonen
               Prime Minister — Kalevi Sorsa
               Legislature — Eduskunta
Political Parties: Social Democrat—54 seats
               People's Democratic League (Communist)—40 seats
               Center—39 seats
               Conservative—35 seats
               Swedish People's—10 seats
               Liberal—9 seats
               Christian League—9 seats
Birth rate: 13.9 per 1,000
Death rate: 9.4 per 1,000
Literacy rate: 99%

Presidents of Finland

1919-1925	Kaarlo Juho Ståhlberg
1925-1931	Lauri Kristian Relander
1931-1937	Per Evind Svinhufvud
1937-1940	Kyösti Kallio
1940-1944	Rysto Heikki Ryti
1944-1946	Carl Gustav Mannerheim
1946-1950	Juho Kusti Pääsikivi
1956-1958	Urho Kekkonen
1958-	Karl August Fagerholm
1958-	Urho Kekkonen

Flag and Coat of Arms

The Finnish flag is a wide blue cross on a white background. The Finnish coat of arms shows a lion (facing left), standing with one paw on the curved scimitar of the oppressor, while in its uplifted mailed fist it brandishes the sword of Finland.

National Anthem

Originally written in Swedish by Johan Ludwig Runeberg and set to music by Fredrik Pacius, the national anthem was entitled "Vårtland." It is given with its English translation, followed by the Finnish version, "Maamme."

Vårtland

Vårt land, vårt land, vårt fosterland
Ljud högt, o dyra ord!
Ej lyfts en höja mot himlens rand
Ej sänks en dal, ej sköljs en strand,
Mer älskad än vår bygd i nord
Än vara faders jord.

Our land, our land, our native land
Oh let her name ring clear.
No peaks against the heavens which stand
No gentle dales or foaming strand
Are loved as we our homes revere
The earth our sires held dear.

Maamme

Oi maamme, Suomi, synnyinmaa
Soi sane kultainen!
Ei laaksoa, ei kukkulaa
Ei vettä, rantaa rakkaampaa
Kuin kotimaa tää pohjoinen
Maa kallis isien.

Selected Bibliography

Aaltio, Maija-Helliki. *Finnish for Foreigners.* Helsinki: Kustannusosa Keyhtiö Otava, 1969.

Bacon, Walter, *Highway to the Wilderness.* New York: Vanguard Press, 1961.

Berry, Erick. *The Land and People of Finland.* New York: J.B. Lippincott Co., 1959.

Bowman, James; Bianco, Margery; and Kolehmainen, Alli. *Tales from a Finnish Tupa.* Chicago: Albert Whitman & Co., 1970.

Bradley, David. *A Lion Among Roses.* New York: Holt, Rinehart and Winston, 1965.

Condon, Richard W. *The Winter War: Russia Against Finland.* New York: Ballantine Books, 1972.

Hinshaw, David. *Heroic Finland.* New York: G.P. Putnam's Sons, 1952.

Irwin, John L. *The Finns and the Lapps.* New York: Praeger Publishers, 1973.

Kakonen, Ulla. *Natural Cooking the Finnish Way.* New York: Quadrangle/New York Times Book Co., 1974.

Kivi, Alexis. *Seven Brothers.* Translated by Alex Matson. New York: Coward McCann, 1929.

Kivikoski, Ella. *Finland.* New York: Frederick A. Praeger, 1967.

Kolehmainen, John. *Epic of the North.* New York Mills, Minn.: North West Publishing Co., 1973.

Lönnrot, Elias. *The Kalevala.* Translated by Francis P. Magoun, Jr. Cambridge, Mass.: Harvard University Press, 1963.

Ojakangas, Beatrice. *The Finnish Cookbook.* New York: Crown Publishers, 1964.

Olin, S.C. *Sauna, the Way to Health.* New York Mills, Minn.: North West Publishing Co., 1963.

Oxenstierna, Eric. *The Norsemen.* Translated by Catherine Hutter. Greenwich, Conn.: New York Graphic Society Publishers, 1965.

Rothery, Agnes. *Finland, the New Nation.* New York: Viking Press, 1936.

Sentzke, Geert. *Finland, Its Church and Its People.* Helsinki: Kirjapaino Oy Lause, 1963.

Simpson, Colin. *The Viking Circle.* New York: William Morrow, 1968.

Sperry, Margaret. *Where Stories Grow.* New York: Crane, Russak & Co., 1977.

Topelius, Zacharias. *Canute Whistlewinks and Other Stories.* Translated by C.W. Foss. London: Longmans, Green & Co., 1927.

Undset, Sigrid. *True and Untrue.* New York: Alfred A. Knopf, 1962.

Vuosikerta, L., ed. *Siirtokansan Kalenteri.* New York Mills, Minn.: North West Publishing Co., 1967.

Wasastjerna, Hans, ed. *History of the Finns in Minnesota.* Translated by Toivo Rosvall. Duluth, Minn.: Minnesota Finnish-American Society, 1957.

Whitney, Arthur. *Teach Yourself Finnish.* London: English Universities Press, 1963.

Aalto, Alvar, 111, 115
Aaltonen, Väinö, 121
Adolphus, Gustavus, 31, 45
Adult education, 152–153
Agricola, Michael, 61, 89–90, 196
Agriculture, 103–105. *See also* Cooperatives
Airlines, 108
Åland Islands, 14, 17, 160
Albert of Mecklenberg, 29
Alcoholism, 96
Alexander I, Czar, 35–36, 97–98
Alexander II, Czar, 34, 121
Alexander II, Pope, 27
Arabia (ceramics), 110–111
Architecture, 113–115
Arctic Circle, 9
Athenaeum, 120
Boating, ice, 138
Bobrikoff, Nickolai Ivanovich, 36–38, 52
Breads, Finnish, 185–188
Budget, national, 145
Cake, Finnish, 193
"Cap of the Four Winds," 81
Ceramics, 110–111
Charms, 70, 87, 156
Children's Choir of Tapiola, 118
Christian II, 30
Christmas, celebration of, 167–168
Christmas ham, 182–183
"Church box," 159
Churches, wooden, 88, 165
Church of Finland. *See* Lutheranism
Civil war, 38–39

Climate, 8–9
Coat of arms, Finnish, 48
Codfish, lye-soaked, 181–182
Communist party, 56
Comprehensive school, 145–148
Consumer products, 109–111
Continuation War, 46–47
Cookies, 192–193, 194
Cooperatives, 107, 212
Crafts, 160–161
Crayfish, cooking of, 180
Cross-country skiing, 135–138
"Cupping woman," 100, 132
Dairying, 104–105
Day care, 57, 146
Design, industrial, 109–111
Dorpat, Treaty of, 39
Downhill skiing, 138
Dress, traditional, 159–160; Lapps, 81
Easter, celebration of, 163–164
Eastern Orthodox Church, 8
Economy, national, 103–111
Edelfelt, Albert, 120
Education, 145–153
Eduskunta, 55
Ehrenstrom, Johann, 113
Ekman, R.V., 120
Emajoki River, 140
Engel, Carl Ludwig, 15, 113–114
Eric IX, 26, 88
Eric XIV, 30–31, 153
Erikson, Leif, 207
Evangelical Lutheran Church. *See* Lutheranism
Evinrude, Ole, 108
Fabrics, 109–110
Fenno-Scandian Shield, 11
Festivals, 161, 165, 166

Finland: army of, 58; arts of, 113–121; Church of, 85, 90, 163; cities of, 15–21; climate of, 8–9; coat of arms of, 48, 215; currency of, 56; economy of, 103–111; education in, 145–153; flag of, 50, 215; forests of, 105; geographic regions of, 13–14; geological formation of, 11; government of, 51–59, 214; Independence Day of, 38–39, 166; language of, 8, 61, 77, 89–90, 197–205; laws of, 56; map of, 12; mortality rates of, 95; name of, 7–8; national anthem of, 116, 215–216; national museum of, 120; prehistory of, 23–26; presidents of, 54–55, 215; Russian rule of, 32, 35–38; Swedish rule of, 26–35; World War II and, 9, 41–49

Finlandia (Sibelius), 116

Finlandia Ski Race, 134, 136

Finlayson, James, 18

Finnglish, 205

Finnish Americans, 168–171, 205, 207–212

Finnish cake, 193

Finnish cooking, 173–195

Finnish Diet (parliament), 36

Finnish language, 8, 61, 77, 89–90, 197–205

Finnrail pass, 108

Finska kakor, 193

Fishing, 108, 138–139, 141

Fish soup, 176–178

Flag, Finnish, 215

Flat bread, 185–186

Folklore, 155–158. *See also* Charms; Holidays

Folk school system, 152

Food, traditional Finnish, 173–195

Forests, economy and, 105–106

Friederich Karl of Hesse, Prince, 53

Fruit soup, 189

Gallen-Kallela, Akseli, 72, 120

Germany, 9, 39, 41, 43–47

Glassware, 110

Government, 51–59. *See also* National budget

Graavilohi, 178

Great Wrath, 32

Haakon VI, 29

Ham, Christmas, 182–183

Häme, 24, 27, 88

Handicraft fairs, 160–161

Hangö, 45, 47, 161

Hannunvaakuna, 92

Hapenleipä, 186

Health services, 95–96

Heimskringla, 87–88

Helsinki, 9, 15–16, 113–114, 141; University of, 16, 97, 151

Helsinki Festival, 118, 165

Henry, Saint, 27, 88

Herännyt, 85

Herring, pickled, 181

Hieroanta, 100–101

Hiltunen, Eila, 112, 121

Hockey, 138

Holidays, 163–168

Ice sports, 138–139

Iitala Glass, 110

Ilmarinen, 65–68, 86

Imatra River, 140

Independence Day, 166
Industrial design, 109-111
Jarl, Birger, 28, 88
Johan (brother of Eric XIV), 31
Joika, 81
Joulukinkku, 182-183
Joulupukki, 167
Juhannus Day, 92, 164-165
Juhannus, Saint, 89
Juusto, 176
Jyväskylä, arts festival of, 165
Kalakeitto, 176-178
Kalakukko, 19, 179-180
Kaleivät, 192-193, 194
Kaleva, 66, 71
Kalevala, 64-73; charms in, 88;
  church opposition to, 91;
  creation of Finland in, 86-87;
  end of shamanism in, 93;
  paintings of, by Akseli Gallen-
  Kallela, 60, 120; sauna de-
  scribed in, 125; skiing men-
  tioned in, 136; works of
  Sibelius based on, 116
Kalevala Day, 163
Kallio, Kyösti, 54
Kangas, Melvin, 117
Kansallispuku, 159-160
Kantele, 63, 91, 117, 154
Karelia, 24, 28, 32, 45-47, 63,
  70, 88
Katiavuori, Ula, 117
Kaustinen Folk Music Festi-
  val, 117, 161, 165
Kekkonen, Urho, 54-55, 143,
  169
Kemi, ski competition at, 136
Kivi, Alexis, 118-119
Knutson, Torgils, 88

Kokkonen, Joonas, 118
Kullervo, 69-70, 116
Kuopio, 19, 136, 165, 166
Kupparimummu, 100, 132
Laestadians, 85
Lahti, 18-19, 106, 136
Lake district, 6, 14, 141
Lake Saimaa, 14, 141
Language, 8, 61, 77, 89-90,
  197-205
Lapland, 9, 21, 47, 75-76; Uni-
  versity of, 151
Lapps, 24, 75-83
Lasimestarinsilli, 181
Leino, Eino, 119
Lemminkäinen, 68, 136
Lihapyöryköitä, 183-184
Linna, Väinö, 119
Lipeä kala, 181-182
Little Christmas pigs (cookies),
  192-193
Log cabins, 25-26, 114, 208
Loggers' competitions, 142,
  165-166
Lönnrot, Elias, 62-64, 72-73,
  91, 97
Louhi, 65-66
Lucia Day, 167
Luoto, Teemo, 121
Lutfisk, 181-182
Lutheranism, 30, 32, 36, 85, 89,
  90, 163, 208
"Maamme," 116, 216
Maaninka, Kaario, 143
Mämmi, 163, 191
Mannerheim, Carl Gustav: civil
  war and, 38; Continuation
  War and, 46; death of, 49;
  early military career of, 42-43;

Memorial Day ceremony and, 166; patriotism and, 49, 56; presidency of, 54, 215; statue of, 50; Winter War and, 44
Mannerheim Line, 44
Margaret of Denmark, 29
Marimekko, 110
Markka (mk.), 56
Masseuse, 100–101
Meat balls, 183–184
Medical care, 57, 95–97, 101
Merchant marine, 108–109
Meri, Veijo, 119
Midsummer, 92, 157, 164–165
Mieto, Juho, 137
Minneapolis, Minnesota, 19
Minnesota, Finnish settlement of, 209, 210
"Molotov bread baskets," 42, 46
Molotov, Vyacheslav M., 41
Monsdatter, Karen, 17, 31
Mortality rates, 95
Music, 115–118. *See also* Festivals
Name days, 171
Names, Finnish, 58, 201, 211
National anthem, 116, 215–216
National budget, 145
National museum, 120
Nicholas II, 36
Nissu nassu, 192–193
Nobel Prizes, 96, 119
Nurmi, Paavo, 121, 142–143
Nuutajarvi Glassworks, 110
Olaf, Saint, 88, 92
Olavinlinna, 19–20, 23, 118
Olympics, 136–137, 142–143
Opera, 117–119

Orthodox Church, 8, 85, 167
Oulu, 20
Oulu Tervakilpailu, 136
Pacius, Fredrik, 117
Paliskunnat, 78–79
Paper production, 106
Parliament. *See* Eduskunta; Finnish Diet
Parvelahti, Unto, 119
Pasty, 184–185
Pennsylvania, Finnish settlement of, 208
Peruskoulu, 145–148
Pesä pällo, 142
Petsamo, 45, 47
Pihkala, Erik, 137
Piirakkaa, 184–185
Pikkujoulu, 166
Pine tar, medicinal uses of, 99
Political parties, 55–56, 214
Pori, jazz festival of, 165
Porkkala, 45
Porse, Knut, 28
Porthan, Henrik Gabriel, 61, 73
Pradzniks, 165
President, duties of, 53
Presidents of Finland, 54–55, 216
Provinces, 13, 57
Puddings, 189–190, 191
Puikkonen, Jari, 137
Pulla, 187–188
Punch (recipe), 194–195
Puukko, 81, 160
Puukkojunkkarit, 20
Pyynikki Open Air Theater, 18, 165
Racing, ice, 139

Railroads, 107–108
Rapids, shooting, 140
Ratia, Armi, 110
Rauma, lace fair of, 160
Rauma Repola Oy, 108
Ravut, 180
Reformation, Protestant, 31, 89–90
Reindeer, 77–82 passim
Reivell, Vilho, 114
Religion, 85–93. *See also* Lutheranism
Rice pudding, 189–190
Rieska, 185–186
Riihivouri, Hilda, 137
Riispuuro, 189–190
Ritvala Helka Festival, 161
Roosevelt, Franklin D., 210
Rose hip soup, 190–191
Rosola, Yrjo, 121
Rovaniemi, 20–21, 47, 83, 115
Ruiskakkuja, 194
Rukatunturi, rapids at, 140
Runeberg, Johan Ludwig, 62, 116, 121
Runeberg, Walter, 121
Rune singers, 63–64, 117
Running, 142–143
Russia: annexation of Finland by, 35–38; cropland ceded to, 103; Finland's present independence of, 54; Finland's role in Sweden's wars against, 28; Finland's role in World War II and, 9, 41–49; Finnish resistance to culture of, 52; Helsinki as capital and, 15; occupation of Finland by, 32; postwar reparations to, 47–48, 108–109; wars of, against Finland, 10
Ruusunmarjakeitto, 190–191
Rya rugs, 109
Rye cookies, 194
Ryti, Risto, 54
Saarinen, Eero, 114–115
Saarinen, Eliel, 114
Saint Urho's Tay, 168–171
Sallinen, Aulis, 118
Salmon, salted, 178
Santa Claus, 167–168
Sauna, 98, 99, 123–133
Savonlinna, 19, 106, 165
Savu sauna, 124–126
Schauman, Eugene, 37–38
School system, 145–153
Sekahedelmäkeitto, 189
Senate Square, 16, 113
Shipbuilding, 108–109
Sibelius Academy, 151
Sibelius, Jean, 72, 115–116
Sillanpää, Frans Eemil, 119
Sillanpää, Müna, 59
Sima, 194–195
Sinberg, Hugo, 120
Sinkonen, Lassi, 120
Sisu, 10
Skating, 138
Skiing, 135–138
Ski Troops, 40, 45, 137
Small Wrath, 32
Smelts in tomato sauce, 179
Soups, 176–178, 189, 190–191
Sourdough, shortcut, 186
Sour rye bread, 186
Soviet Union. *See* Russia
Sports, 135–143
Squeaky cheese, 176

Stählberg, Kaarlo Juho, 53
Stockholm Bloodbath, 30
"Study Circles," 152–153
Suicide, 95
Suomalainen, 8
Suomenlinna, 16
Suomi, 8, 24
Suomi College, 212
Sweden, 26–35, 44, 47, 52, 88
Sweet bread, 187–188
Swimming, 139–140
Takalo, Helena, 137
Tampere, 14, 17–18, 165
Tapio, 72, 87
Tapiola, 16, 87, 114; Children's
    Choir of, 118
Tapiovarra, Tapio, 120
Tarmakers, 20, 106
Taulan-Antti, 157–158
Textiles, 109–110
Thomas, Saint, 17, 28
Three Crowns, 29
Toermaenen, Jouko, 137
Tomaatisilakat, 179
Topelius, Zachris, 156
Transportation, 107–108
Treaty of Dorpat, 39
Tsasounas, 165
Turi, Johan, 75
Turku, 15, 16–17, 90, 113,
    160–161, 165; cathedral of,
    17, 88, 90; University of, 90,
    97, 151

Turunen, Heikki, 120
United States, 46, 48–49, 114,
    205, 207–212
Universities, 151; Helsinki, 16,
    97, 151; Turku, 90, 97, 151
University education, 151–152
Urho, Saint, 168–171
U.S.S.R. *See* Russia
Väätainen, Juha, 143
Väinämöinen, 23, 64–70, 72,
    86–87, 93, 117
Valio, 104
Vappu, 164
"Vårtland," 116, 215
Vasa, Gustavus, 15, 30, 32, 89
Verin, Lasse, 143
Viili, 105, 174, 175
Vikings, 24–25, 207
Virtanen, A.I., 96
Vocational education, 149–151
Voileipäpöyta, 172, 173–174
Waltari, Mika, 119
Welfare, 56
Winter Olympics (1980), 136–
    137
Winter War, 44–45, 119
Wizards, 72, 76, 86, 92. *See also*
    Väinämöinen
Women, status of, 58–59
Wood products, 106
World War I, 38
World War II, 9, 41–49
Yachts, 108, 140